GETTING IN

DR. NORRY KALER BSc MSc MD

2015

1st Edition

ABOUT THE AUTHOR

Hi, My name is Dr. Norry Kaler and I'm honoured that this book ended up in your hands either in print copy, or your ipad, iphone, kindle, speakers as an audiobook, or whatever technology you have. I have always been a strong believer in community and supporting one another for the greater benefit. My goal with this book is to educate you and prevent you and your family from making the mistakes I made.

I'm a medical doctor who is living in Calgary, Alberta, Canada. I'm a father of two young girls who are my pride and joy. My best friend, and mentor was my father, Iqbal Singh Kaler, who passed in 2006. He was a silent gentle warrior that I wish to become. His life was enriched by giving to others and living simply. It is his morals and values that live in me and are now providing you with this resource.

I completed my undergraduate degree in Chemistry from the University of Northern British Columbia, and a masters degree from the University of Alberta. I then completed some training at Mount Saint Vincent University in Halifax. I completed my medical school training at Dalhousie University in Halifax, Nova Scotia. Between some of these degrees I had my own business helping pre-medical students and high school student prepare for university and medical school admissions. This research guided me into medical school, and finally today to you.

Sit back and relax. Don't fasten your seatbelt, just enjoy the ride.

Dr. Norry Kaler
Suite 850 - 743 Railway Ave
Canmore, AB
T3B 4X2
DrKaler@braidacademy.com

ISBN-13: 978-1519333759

ISBN-10: 1519333757

DEDICATION

This book is dedicated to the person in the gym who asked me how to get into medical school. So many asked, but you triggered this writing. I only hope you will have the courage to follow your dreams and slay your fears.

To my father, Iqbal Singh Kaler, my mother, Harjit Kaur Kaler, and to my children Havah Kaler and Nalah Kaler, may you grow up to be "strong and brave" like your Grandpa.

This book is also dedicated to you, the reader. I hope you gain from it, not only advice for your future career in health care, but also for your life.

Be motivated. Be a Leader. Work hard. Take Action.

ACKNOWLEDGEMENTS

Thank you to the few people in my life that continue to allow me to dream. So many say it can't be done. So many stop dreaming because of fear. We must learn to swim in our pain and happiness and be grateful for both experiences equally. It is our darkness that helps us grow and *see* the light.

Thank you to Monique and Ted for being supportive and listening to me dream, and for your openness and support. Monique - thank you for taking the time to edit this book, Thank you to Cale for providing a lonely man with a home. To Sarah for always encouraging me to walk into the light and to not be afraid of greatness. To Sharona, for being part of so much of my life and teaching me to rise like a salmon.

TABLE OF CONTENTS

Introduction

Chapter 1 - What is it going to take?
        My motivational speech to you.

Chapter 2 - When to start thinking about medical school?
        Parents read this chapter.

Chapter 3 - Why medical school? Is it really worth it?

Chapter 4 - For the immigrant parent and child

Chapter 5 - Private schools vs public vs home schooling

Chapter 6- Choosing an undergraduate degree

Chapter 7 - Choosing your state or province of study

Chapter 8 - Statistics - you're not going to like it

Chapter 9 - Medical school admissions an overview

Chapter 10 - Extra - curricular experiences.

Chapter 11 - MCAT

Chapter 12 - Money matters

Chapter 13 - The application

Chapter 14 - The interview process

Chapter 15 - Getting rejection letters

Chapter 16 - Deciding to go abroad for medicine

Chapter 17 - Special Populations and Circumstances

Chapter 18 - Medical school You did it!

Chapter 19 - Residency

Chapter 20 - VACATION! Summer time what to do?

Chapter 21 - You're done!

Introduction

<u>You applied how many times?</u>

"If I had to cut a tree down in 8 hours I would spend 6 hours sharpening my axe. "

~ Abraham Lincoln

Before I begin, I want to let you know that I am honoured that you are reading this book and are open to listening to my story. I am also honoured that you are considering me as someone who may be able to help you on your journey. I want to help you. I believe in you. You may ask - why? How? You don't even know me? I do know that you have greatness in you. We all do. It's just that very few of us are willing to put in the hard work and dedication needed to achieve our dreams. It's not everyday that we pick up a book or talk to someone who truly cares about our success. I know I didn't have someone like that in my life other than my mother and father. I hope this book will act as that support to you when you need it most. This book is not only about getting into medical school or a health professions program. It is about you. It is about believing in yourself. Searching your heart for what you REALLY want. It's not going to be easy, but every dream takes hard work and it needs to be worth it. By the end of this book you need to decide - is this worth it for me?

<u>Who am I?</u>

My name is Norry Kaler. I'm a medical doctor who got into medical school at age 30 after being rejected 44 times over 8 years. In those 8 years I lost my father to critical illness, my daughters were both diagnosed with medical conditions at age 1 and nearly died, I took care of my mother who was depressed since my father passed, and I separated from my wife of 13 years whom I love very much. I can tell you from experience, I know what it is like to hurt. I have been there. It was hard, it is hard, but I didn't give up. There was a voice inside me that kept whispering to keep going - even against all odds. In a place even deeper inside me I found my character and my dreams that lay dormant for so long. I didn't have the support of people. No one believed in me, few supported me, and even fewer encouraged me. Worst of all, people gave me the wrong advice and I believed them. I'm thankful, when I look back, that I had the strength to accept the pain - not fight it or push it away – it took warrior-like courage. I learned how to turn all the rejection and pain into a "bring it on - I'll push harder" mentality. Now my passion is to help others break open doors - to crush secrets that people withheld from me and are also withholding from you - to give you an opportunity to dream again like you did as a child and to never give up. Mostly, I want you to not have to suffer and waste money like I did because I lacked the proper guidance.

My story is one of a little boy, an only child, born of immigrant parents, that faced tremendous adversity, and never gave up. Today I stand humbled by my experience and passionate to share my story and lessons with you. The story I told you was not exactly something I liked talking about until this year (2015). Now, I have opened myself up to share things I haven't shared with many people, because I now realize that I have a choice… A choice to help you, your family, and your future generations.

11My parents emigrated from India in 1976 and lived in low income housing because they had no money. My father had a heart condition caused by having strep throat as a child. It wasn't treated because the poor village he grew up in had no penicillin. Four of his friends there died. Though he survived, he had complications. His heart became enlarged and he developed rheumatic fever. For the remainder of his young life he was stable, but when the government of Canada found out that he had immigrated to Canada with a heart condition, the police randomly showed up at the door one day, handcuffed him and sent him back to India. I wasn't born at the time, but that story still gets me all welled up. Imagine coming to a new country with hopes and dreams, wanting to build a future for your family and then getting put in a police cruiser and getting sent back to India while your wife remained in Canada. Six months later, he was able to return to Canada after finally getting a clean bill of health.

The next year, my parents worked in various laborious jobs. Mom was hired to cut loose threads at the Levi's factory - although she had an Education degree from India. Dad scored in the top 1% of Indians on the State Engineering exams and was a successful engineer. In Canada, this qualified him for a job selling vacuum cleaners at Sears. In the evenings he would work as a parking attendant at a hospital parking lot. He had a turban at the time and in the 1970's in Canada, racism was rampant. People would say racial slurs to his face - things that I can't mention here.

Dad realized he needed a change. Together, he and mom decided he needed to go back to school in Canada. With no money for tuition, they had to move into a house with five families in a rough inner-city neighbourhood. Rent was $80 per month. My mom worked morning and night shifts to help put him through school. She tells a story of her freezing on a - 30 below night. She couldn't afford a proper winter jacket and was wearing a thin coat. Men approached her thinking she was a prostitute.

Dad finished his Masters of Engineering degree at the University of Manitoba at the top of his class. He received a large scholarship, allowing him and mom to move into a small apartment. Then they had me, their only child. Unfortunately, things got worse before they got better. He now couldn't get a job because of his turban and beard. He had grown his hair long his entire life. When he had it cut at the barber, he cried, remembering his mother washing and grooming it since he was a child. As the hair fell, he realized he was willing to do whatever it took to succeed. The rest is history. He got a job at a prominent company, SNC Lavalin, slowly worked his way up to Senior Engineer, and travelled the world for work.

What I learned from this story, and the reason I share it is, life is hard. Some people have it tougher than others. However, those who take this difficulty and rise above it become virtually unstoppable. They rise to any challenge. I learned this not from my mom and dad's work ethic - but merely by their story. They didn't bring it up more than once or twice, but when I heard it - it was locked in. When I struggled to get into medical school after Dad died and I had no support - I thought of them struggling. *If he could do it, so could I.*

I applied to medical school eight years running, I started in 2002 and was accepted in 2010. That is forty seven applications in Canada over eight years, 44 rejection letters, 3 interviews and one acceptance to Dalhousie Medical School. I still have those rejection letters as a reminder of my achievement. I started applying at age 22. My girlfriend at the time got in at 23 and was done medical school and residency by the time I started. That's just to give you an idea of how hard this process can be. Imagine being rejected year after year while watching everyone around you enjoy medical school. I don't want you to have to go through this; I want to help you focus your energy in the right direction, with the right plan. It's going to be hard, but if I can do it, you can do it.

"Life is hard - Either we can work hard now and relax later or relax now and struggle later - It's up to you."

~Les Brown

Now just in case you read too fast, please take a few minutes to re-read the previous section. Absorb it. I'll ask you about it later in the book. I'm going to ask you if you have that kind of passion. Drive. Determination. If yes, then not only are you going to make an excellent physician, you are going to be someone I want to get to know. Someone inspiring. A leader. When you believe in something, you have to give it everything you have, no matter what. No matter what anyone says, no matter what your mind says, I'm here to tell you to believe, go for your dreams, and never give up.

Be relentless.

Yes...I cried, I suffered, I lost my father and got depressed. Both my children were diagnosed with chronic medical conditions at the tender age of 1, I separated from my wife, went broke, moved across the country 4 times, lived in 11 different houses and blah blah blah.

The only thing you need to ask me now is - was it worth it? I'm sitting next to my canoe in the mountains writing this book and feeling - it was 100% worth it. A feeling I will never be able to describe to anyone, but I know one thing: I'm proud of me and that I didn't give up. Finishing medical school ignited a fire in me to believe more strongly in myself, to go for my dreams, and to not care what other people think. I respect and trust who I am. I want the same for you.

So how did I get in? Well, after 7 years of listening to every-one - friends, family, internet forums, guidance counsellors, medical school advisors, bartering with God (If I get in I will…), and none of it working - I knew I had to change some-thing. This is what this book is about - sharpening your axe like, Abraham Lincoln said - not just spending hours wasting your energy and diminishing your spirit.

I'm teaching you what I spent seven years doing wrong and what I spent 1 year doing right. I stopped listening to every-one, did a tremendous amount of research on all the medical schools in Canada, US and abroad - their entrance requirements, their prerequisites, statistics on admissions and failures - and made a plan of action. I decided to become an expert in admissions. I spent 4 months of that 8th year compiling every last bit of data on what it would take to get in. And this is what I am sharing with you.

What this book is NOT!

No, I'm not going to make you buy six more books and then have you call some 1-900 number to get the secret. Nope,

I'm completely open, and all my information is yours. Think of it as my way of saying "screw you" to all the naysayers out there, all the Princeton Review, Kaplan, and other review companies, horrible guidance counsellors, etc. - all out there to steal your money, and misguide you. Yes, I said it. University admission to professional programs, and recruitment to these schools is a billion dollar industry. Think I'm joking? Later in the book I get into the numbers of it all.

I spent $48,500 trying to get into medical school, not including lost wages and costs of living. Students who helped write a chapter on studying abroad talk about the thousands of students spending $300,000 - $500,000 on medical school in Australia with no guarantee of being able to get a residency spot in Canada. Where is that money going? In the pockets of all those universities – it's all business, my friends.

Why other medical school admissions and university guidance books suck.

There are three books currently in press on the topic and all are outdated and laced with poor advice. Medical schools are very dynamic and change yearly. A book written in 2006 is now practically obsolete.

Telling you the admissions criteria isn't an issue - any one of you can look this up online in minutes. The issue is learning from someone who has experience, someone who knows the system. The problem is - you don't know how to decipher what is good information from bad yet because you're on the other side - you're looking for help. This is where I get upset - because I was too and these kinds of books lead me astray.

Another example of bad advice is an author who wrote about how one should choose a university. The author mentions students should choose courses that interest them at a university that inspires them, and that they should speak to guidance counsellors and ask their opinion. This is the farthest thing from the truth.

After taking a breath, I'm now going to tell you what bullshit this is. You have to decide if you want to go to medicine. Period. If you don't know, read this book. At the end of the book - if you don't know - throw it out or put it on the shelf until you're ready. You can't just wing it and hope for the best. You need a game plan. You can't pick a university based on "feelings". You have to pick any school - even a dump - based on the chance it will give you to succeed and get into medical school.

Come on people - either you take this seriously or you end up as one of the 18,000 applicants a year who do not get in to medical school in Canada. Do you want to be one of the 2000 students that make it? If so, take it SERIOUSLY. If medical school admissions are not based on feelings but quantitative data and points from your application, then you should be doing what it takes to get more points.
I will walk you through how to choose an undergraduate degree and where you should look. That is why I broadened this book to talk about Dentistry, Pharmacy, Nursing, and other health care professions.

I know I sound opinionated and direct, but I want your life to be easier than mine. I want other books and authors who have no idea what they are talking about to be crushed, since it is all leading you away from your journey to success.

I like to use the example of a personal trainer. When I go to the gym to work out and a personal trainer doesn't look great or like I want to look, I laugh. How can someone who doesn't look fit and strong have the balls to tell me what to do? It's hypocritical. How come all the weight loss books are written by people who have never been obese themselves? That's why they don't work.

Same logic applies here - I have credibility because of the amount of times I have applied to medical school and the extensive research I had to put into my own life - I'm now offering you that. You can trust me. Just read the book and see how you feel. If you feel like I have good points to offer then follow them, if not - don't.

Learning from my mistakes so you don't make them

After I gathered all the data on medical schools, I then began compiling what I systematically needed to do. I considered it a research project. I then met with deans of admissions (the people in charge of admissions at medical schools) from various universities and learned what they needed from me. Many of them told me things I didn't know about my application - like I needed to do a year of upgrading, or that my Masters degree counted for 1 mark out of 100 possible application points. "That was a waste of 2.5 years", I thought.

What did I do? I did 1 year of upgrading at a small college and got a 4.0 (A+ average). I applied, got three interviews to four schools and got in. Basically, I had not gotten interviews for 7 years, but after 1 year of systematic analysis of what was needed from me, I got results. Now that was sharpening my axe!

Getting into med school was one of the happiest days of my life. After 8 years and 44 rejections, the victory was that much sweeter. I completed my degree in 4 years averaging 80-90% on all my exams, and scoring in the top 15% of all Canadian medical students in Canada on my LMCC (National medical exam at the end of medical school that all students write). Not so bad for someone who got rejected 44 time!. I actually started to think I was dumb after getting rejected so much, but I knew deep inside that I was able to do anything if I put my heart to it. It is my vision to prevent you from a majority of this pain. Of course it is going to be hard, of course you're going to have hard days. If you feel there are not many people on your team, that's ok. The most important thing is for you to believe in yourself!

Let me tell you another story...

Have you heard the story of the 4-minute mile? For almost a century no human being had been able to run a mile in less than 4 minutes. The day that one person did it - Roger Bannister - something happened. All of a sudden more and more people were able to do it, and today tens of thousands of people have broken the 4-minute mile. Is that because we are stronger now, have better food, and have better shoes? No. It's because Roger Bannister believed he could do it, and he opened the door for people to believe that they could do it. Do you see the power of belief and faith in yourself? I had to find that belief in myself. All you need is a plan, a lot of sweat, and most of all, faith in yourself. If I can do it, so can you.

I'm here for you - all for you.

Are you ready? Let's do this.
Sincerely yours,

Dr. Norry Kaler BSc, MSc, MD

DrKaler@BRAIDAcademy.com

Chapter 1 - What is it going to take?
My motivational speech to you.

If you didn't read the introduction - go back and read it - it talks about how I got into medical school - and you don't want to miss my story.

Okay sit down, here is the first bit of tough love you're going to get from me. I know it's fast and it's the first paragraph of the first chapter of my first book. Shit that's a lot of firsts. I think many of you reading this book have the strength it takes to be successful in life, but many of you won't do what is required to win. I know you believe it in your heart, deep inside. The reason I say this is that today's world is full of distractions. Texting, internet, TV, girls, boys, drugs, sex, clothes, cars, sports - and the list goes on. We live in the age of distractions. We have access to more information, food, and products now than ever in history.

We also suck more now then we've ever sucked before. We are so lazy and full of excuses. We're always waiting for the next iPhone, the next car, the next relationship, the next best thing. We don't take the time to get to know ourselves, to see what we're truly made of. This is why many of you will give up on your path. You will try to find another way out - going abroad to the Caribbean, Ireland, Hungary, for medical school, or giving up and get that job at the local coffee shop you always wanted (sorry for the sarcasm).

I want you to be pissed off right now. Angry, fired up and ready to go to battle.

Then go to youtube and search "Nobody owes you anything - by Les Brown and Beats Reloaded".

Are you done? Did you skip this? Then you probably are like many people. You don't pay attention and you're going to give up. FOCUS and go watch the video.

This book is not only going to help you on your educational journey, but it's going to be a way to restructure your mind, your life, and get yourself back. Trust me - when you're 35, 50, 80 - you're going to wish you had done this now.

If you're a North American, you should know one of my favourite speakers - Kevin O'leary of O'leary Funds. This billionaire tycoon could be sitting in the Bahamas getting fat and doing nothing important with his life. But he isn't. He is working his butt off, reconnecting with his family after learning life's lessons and being honest about his journey. He doesn't give a stink about what you think, and that is why he is successful in his own way - and when he looks in the mirror (I haven't looked in the mirror with him, but I'm assuming he would agree) that he is proud of his achievements and feels thankful for his experience - like I do mine.

I only wish everyone could also look in the mirror and be proud of their journey - the bad and the good.

After all the garbage I've been through I know that worrying about others isn't going to get you places. You are going to have to dig deep down and become the warrior that you know you are. If you don't want to go to battle, don't want to work hard, sweat, and cry - throw out this book now! Stop wasting your time reading this!

But…If you are on board, then read books and listen to videos from motivational people. Don't worry if you don't know what we are saying. Just listen. I have no clue what Kevin is saying half the time, but his charisma, his vision, and belief in himself are exactly the same principles I have in my life. I never give up, and no one - not even Kevin O'leary, will ever out-work me. No one. I want you to believe the same thing.

So now that you're fired up, lets get to work!

Start with this. Say this out loud - If you're in a coffee shop - who cares - no one knows you anyway…Just say it dammit!

I am not going to make any excuses. I'm going to go for my dreams, and I'm going to believe in myself. I'm going to depend on me. I'm going to take ACTion!

For those of you who didn't say this out loud, check yourself right now. If you can't even do this, what are you going to do when medical school says 'no'? What are you going to do when one of your parents dies? Are you going to have some courage then? If you couldn't do a simple thing like this now, that means you care too much about what other people think, and if you do - then you were like the old Dr. Norry Kaler, and you're not going to be successful. You can't give a crap about anyone. Once you set your dream in place - lock it in and ROCK it!

For all you ladies out there - I can't stress enough how pertinent this is to you. As a father of two young girls, I spend five minutes a day getting them pumped up and motivated. Women are the reason this planet hasn't blown up. You have kept us together - supporting us men for far too long, but now it's your turn to help turn things around. It's time for women to suit up and get ready for battle - because it is you who are the leaders of tomorrow. Believe in yourself. Dream.

Let's get started.

Chapter 2 - When to start thinking about medical school or professional programs? Parents read this chapter.

Immigrant Parents

I know some of you who are applying will be thinking "why is this guy talking about parents?" Well, for a good sum of parents out there - Asian, Eastern European, Indian, African, or almost all immigrant parents want their children to have a successful professional job. This is mainly because they don't want them to have to do the laborious jobs that many of them had to after they emigrated. Education is a major priority for many of these immigrant families - not to say it isn't in North American families. The level of attention and priority of education in a typical immigrant family is similar to a North American family's priority of sports, socializing, and outdoor activities. By the 2nd generation, this tends to change, with this generation assimilating the North American ways. Personally, I believe in a balance between the eastern and western ways.

My immigrant parents came to Canada overqualified and unable to work in their Education and Engineering professions. Many of the taxi drivers and minimum wage immigrant labour employees in North America were doctors, engineers, and educators in their country, but could not get a job in their field because their qualifications were not recognized here. For many it was too hard to go back to school and repeat their education over again because they had children and a family to support on minimum wage income. Many immigrants who went back to school to re-qualify their education found those early years extremely hard, but the rest of their lives was smoother and forever changed due to their success.

Of course non-immigrant parents want the best for their children and understand the value of education too, many of them also having to work laborious jobs to support their families. Many of the students to whom I provide guidance are non-immigrant physicians who have been out of medical school for 10-20 years and want to learn how to navigate the education system for their children that has changed dramatically since they were in university.

This chapter will especially benefit parents and help families looking for advice on medical school and guidance on university programs. The valuable tips and lessons I provide can be used in so many different avenues of life. Many parents just say "it takes hard work to succeed - so just suffer through it no matter what happens..." I do believe in the hard work component, but it needs to be effective and guided with laser-like precision. For many, the educational journey needs to be moulded to the unique situations that arise in all of our lives. I often hear from parents, "My kid just needs to work harder." Okay maybe this is true, but work harder at what... Their biochemistry degree at a large university? You will see that this is the last program your child should sign up for.

There needs to be short and long term goal setting, and an overall vision. Not having goals, dreams, and a plan is why so many people are unsuccessful in life, and education is no different. You can never start too early.

Physician Parents

I get numerous questions from physicians who are parents and looking to get their children into medical school. This was another reason I wrote this book - for you doctor parents as well.

Many people wonder why there are so many medical students that have parents who are doctors. Do they have a secret? Is there some sneaky way to get in? 99% of the time there is no "sneaky" way to get in and there are a few loop holes. I'm not going to address that in this book because you shouldn't be thinking about these rare circumstances and tricks. If you are a dean of medicine or have an influential role in the faculty at a medical school please feel free to contact me as you do have an edge compared to your peers - you are part of that 1%.

Back to explaining why so many medical students are 2nd, 3rd or even 4th generation doctors. Medicine is a special vocation. It is a profession that offers not only financial freedom and stability, but it is a profession that has earned the respect of society. Not many professions have established and retained this respect. Personally, I have noticed that people are more trusting, inquisitive, attentive, and look up to me as a leader. Medicine provides credibility that not many other professions can provide. It is an extremely rewarding profession that remunerates individuals very well for caring for the sick. Making between $250,000 to $1,000,000 depending on your specialty for helping people is something that physicians have become accustomed to. They want that same lifestyle and respect for their children as well and this motivates them to encourage their children to pursue a similar career.

"But I don't know how to help my child!"

I had little help from my parents because they didn't know how to navigate the maze of university and applications to medical school. I knew I wanted to go to medical school after my dad had open-heart surgery because of Rheumatic Fever as a child. When he died in the Intensive Care Unit, I knew I wanted to change things. That is why medicine became my passion. My mother didn't know what to do either - she was a typical immigrant stay-at-home mom who did everything for the family on the home front. Things outside the home relating to finances were my father's responsibility. Raising me was a joint venture - not always easy.

I had to learn everything on my own - which was very difficult. My father wasn't there to help me through the medical school process but I know he was there in spirit. My book will help parents who don't have a clue - and are listening to so many people who don't have a clue - or their advice is not relevant today. My goal is to especially help parents. If you're wondering why, I have always been a "helper" - someone who thrives off the success of others and my vision involves you and your family succeeding. Isn't that the point of humanity? To help one another? To give back a lesson you have learned?

Medical school is not like it used to be. This chapter is for you, parents, and as well as those of you students who are starting to read this book in high school and got this book from a friend or family member. If you are already in university - read this chapter anyway to make sure you don't miss any major concepts.

For Students

DIAMOND - Don't Go to a Large Prestigious University. Go to a small college or university.

When should you start getting serious about medical school? I believe this is in high school. For you doctor parents, students already at a large university, medical students, sorry if this Diamond gets you off track or if you disagree. My job is to be honest and provide you with advice that will work - not that "feels" good.

Universities are businesses; one of their priorities is to make money. Many of them have excellent professional programs and research institutes, however that doesn't change the fact that they are there to make money. If they don't make money - their professors and staff don't get paid, and they don't survive. So many parents may be upset or anxious right now, or have decided to throw this book out, but listen up - this may be the best Diamond of them all that may help you get in. No medical school application that I know of, gives you admission points for coming from a large university. It's simply not possible and it's not ethical. The admissions committees don't care what university you went to. If I'm wrong then show me the evidence.

Medical schools and professional programs often have pre-requisites (a few don't and many schools are moving towards fewer required courses). Pre-requisites are courses you need to complete in order to be eligible to apply. Many medical schools require an undergraduate degree. Yes, I know some schools allow entry after three years of undergraduate programming, but they are very few and the competition is fierce. Many universities don't require a science degree; my girlfriend at the time had an Arts degree in First Nations studies. Not once did that come up in the application - and in fact, the diversity of her degree actually helped her stand out from her competition. She got in.

My main point: go to a small college or university with small class sizes (no more than 40 in a class), and frankly, choose a college that has all the sports jocks and people who couldn't get into larger universities. You don't need to be competing with the people who want to build another part of the NASA space station. You also don't want to get an 85% on your test and get a C because you were "curved" or compared against everyone else in your class. Yes this happens. If you had an 85% on an exam in a class of 200 and the class average was 95% - you will get a C or D depending on the standard deviation of scores. That's just not fair in my mind. Small colleges and universities won't curve scores if there are only 30 students in a class. So why not give yourself the best chance? Is it because you want to tell people "I got an undergrad from McGill or UBC?" At the end of the day, if you're working at a fast food restaurant after spending $30,000 in school, was it worth it? I hope not.

Summary: go to a smaller school.

Now you need to make sure your college or university is a degree granting institution and has a four-year program. That is the best so you don't have to switch schools after two years. There are many colleges that have two-year programs and then you can transfer to a larger university and finish your degree there, but that requires a lot of work, convincing schools that classes you took are the same as what they offer.

Some school won't recognize your grades, others will try to lower your scores because you had a small class - yes I have heard of this, etc. etc. Try to go to a school for 4 years - get your awesome grades and get your degree.

Grades

This leads me to my next Diamond - grades. Grades do matter and it may be the most important aspect of your application to get you an interview.

DIAMOND - GRADES DO MATTER! - Just accept it, and get awesome grades!

I used to believe that maybe if my community service, volunteering or work with Aboriginal communities would count for an equal amount as my grades. That was a "feeling" I had. It was the farthest thing from the truth. Most medicals schools use algorithms (mathematical formulas) to keep things objective and fair. The best way to keep things fair is to start by comparing people based on their grades. After all, grades are just numbers and what easier way is there to separate thousands of applications?

This is why I suggest you to go to a smaller school. Let me use Mt. St. Vincent University in Halifax as an example. There is an average of 30 students per undergraduate class with many having only 15. You go there and do a degree in Nutrition. You get a 4-year degree with great grades because you worked hard and your teachers were able to get to know you and see your work ethic. You apply to medicine with your excellent grades and this now becomes an asset on your application - not a liability.

The flip side is what I did. I went to the University of Alberta did in a BSc in Chemistry. I was a 90% high school student, I got 65% average in my first semester of university and I dropped out. Looking back, dropping out was one of the best decisions I made. Many people would have pushed on and finish their degree and "hoped" they would somehow get in. The problem is that after sucking at one semester it's pretty easy to get down and suck at another semester and another, until you graduate with a B, C, or D average. The problem now is that you have 4 years of crappy grades. I had 350 students in my first year sciences classes. I'd say 80% of them wanted to go to medical school. That's intimidating in itself. My dropping out meant I had a bad semester of grades, not 4 years of bad grades.

After taking the year off - I went to a smaller school - got better grades - an A average - until I registered in a 400-level cancer research project (highest level of undergraduate training - usually courses taken in the final year will be 400 level. 100 for first year, 200 for 2nd year and so on). I wanted to do a cancer research project as I "felt" it would look good on my resume. I thought the interview committee would think - "Wow look this guy did cancer research." No evidence, no guidance, no plan. I just kept hoping and was winging it.

As fate would have it, this teacher had it out to roast me - but didn't tell me until the last month. I had spent 3 years building my grades back up to an A average until... drum roll please - the professor in charge of this project game me a C- in the last month of my degree in a research project which took over 1.5 years to complete. This plummeted my GPA (Grade Point Average - average of all the marks you have received in all the courses you have taken). But wait, it gets worse. He told me that he had wanted to be a doctor in Australia and that, as he couldn't get in, he became a cancer researcher in Canada. He then went on to tell me that I should be a salesman, not a doctor. I cried, called my parents who were livid. Then I called my girlfriend and tried to make a plan of what I should do. Looking back - the hardest part of this experience was not the grades being affected, but more the discrimination and negative impact that this man had on my self esteem. This is another reason why I provide the next diamond.

DIAMOND - *Take objective courses - courses where hard work = grades.*

Courses that are subjective are dangerous. In these types of courses the professor has a say in your grades. If they don't like you, they can give you a lower grade and look for flaws in your work. Courses that are objective have clear outlines. You can do well in them if you meet the objectives and excel in them. If the teacher challenges this - you can prove your effort with evidence of your grades, and documented achievement of your objectives. Examples of objective courses are: physiology, anatomy, physics, math, biology, most nursing courses, pharmacy courses, and nutrition courses, etc.

I realized that medical schools not only look at grades, but your progression of grades. Many of them weigh the last 2 years of schooling more than the first 2 years. For me. that meant disaster, hence the 44 rejections - mostly due to this one ass, and me not knowing what to do to change this. I kept "hoping" that it would work out. I don't want you to hope, but to have a plan and some goals. If you don't get in - I want the reason to be because you didn't work hard enough, you didn't push, that you gave up. Not because you didn't know what to do.

DIAMOND - *If you haven't gotten in after 2 attempts you need to change something in your application. Grades, MCAT, reference letters, interview prep - etc.*

If you didn't get in like me - that's okay. Life is hard. You must accept this. You have to take what it gives you and keep moving forward. Never give up the fight on your dreams until your breath is gone. For me. this meant not giving up after that stinky cancer researcher tried to change my life. I never gave up, and eventually I accomplished my dream, and now I'm able to help you. You can brush it off your shoulders, get back up, get in and then send any naysayers a present. I sent this researcher a signed copy of this book. I'm stronger now because of the challenges and because it has been hard.

Bad Advice

I had a lot of "bad" advice on my application journey but I don't dwell on why I got all that bad advice.   Now, I have a purpose - to help you and future generations plan your education.

Without any advice or direction from someone who knew what they were talking about I listened to guidance counsellors and friends who said I should do a graduate degree as it would probably help. Graduate degrees are Masters or Doctor of Philosophy degrees (MSc/ PhD). This person was in medical school so I thought he knew what he was talking about. The guidance counsellor was also a professor in the faculty of medicine, but not a medical doctor. I decided to do my Masters degree at the University of Alberta. There was a researcher there who did excellent work with Aboriginal people and diabetes. I had found a new interest in Aboriginal health and I thought this could be fun, and "may" also help me get into medical school. Nope. I did my MSc, published a few articles and applied, over and over - not even an interview. Why did I do the MSc? Because some doctors and some medical students told me it would be a good idea. Yes, you heard me - I trusted people who had no clue! I begged people, sucked up, took people out for coffee, to try to figure out some secret. It never revealed itself. People kept telling me to give up, start another job, try something else because they felt sorry for me, and I could see their lack of belief in me. I still had no focused plan - no one to help guide me. To make things worse I found out that the MSc is actually worth only 1 point out of 100 possible points on my application. Once again, I felt like I had wasted my time. Another 2.5 years had passed.

As I mentioned before, I researched medical schools and stopped listening to friends and others who didn't have a clue. I went to a smaller school and did a year of upgrading. I got a near perfect GPA and got in. This year of upgrading showed the medical school committee that I had made changes to my application, continuously trying to improve it. I showed them that I could do a full course load. I boosted my GPA with nine A+'s and one A during the year, and my progression of grades in the last two years looked great and I finished strong. Most importantly, I also showed myself that I could do great in school, and that I had not given up.

In summary, grades matter, and the progression of grades matter. Obviously, try to get the best grades you can the entire way through, but if you have a choice - finish strong. Impress your teachers, work hard, go for it. Get that A/A+ average that you deserve.   Go to a smaller school.

For Parents and Students

If you're a high school or university student, circle this chapter and my introduction and FORCE your parents to read these if they haven't yet. You may be surprised to hear this but if your parents support you during this process, it is going to be a lot easier. If you're now the parent reading this - congratulations! Welcome to my book. Think of me as a guide, helping your child and family become successful. University guidance is a tricky business. Many are looking out for their own wellness and keeping secrets so that others don't get ahead. I'm not like that and frankly, that's why I think parents out there should read this entire book. It's short and will teach you some of the hurdles that may stand in your young adult's way.

Every journey should have a guide to help along the way. I only want the best for your family and future generations. Let me be your guide. It's about time the world produces some authentic people who are out there to serve first and gain second. Too many leaders have let me down by gaining first and serving second. Their priorities are backwards from mine.

When should you start thinking about medical school or other health professions? As early as you can! Start saving money now for your kid's education. It's going to be expensive. The average cost of medical school today is around $125,000 and I think that's a low estimate. Don't worry banks are happy to help once you have an admissions letter. For more information on finances and how much it will cost - please see the chapter on "Money".

Elementary / High School

Our public and private school models for grades 1 to 12 suck. Yes, you heard me - most boarding and private schools I've been to are just not up to par. Public schools have become a daycare for children and private schools are no better once you take into account paying $20,000 to $50,000 per year. Is it really $20,000 better than public schools - heck no. I've gone to Switzerland and seen the top boarding schools there. Currently the top eight boarding schools in the world are in Switzerland - again I was unimpressed and shocked by the $140,000 per year price tag. Now don't get me wrong, I don't have the slightest issue with paying $50,000 or even $100,000 for my child's schooling if I knew it provided the service I was looking for. Medical school doesn't provide housing, food, sports, quality education or teach life lessons and it costs $20,000 per year. So, no, I don't have a problem with investing in my kids now. People blow $10,000 on a vacation 2 -3 times per year, buy a $50,000 - $100,000 vehicle every few years. Is your kid not worth more than your vehicle or your $500,000 house?

I believe that nothing should be taught to our precious kids unless there is a valid reason for it. Everything we teach our children should be evaluated, scrutinized, and have a purpose. The rest of the time should be reserved for play and imagination. Kids are supposed to learn and have fun while learning. If they are not having fun they are going to hate what they are doing. We want learning to be fun, directed, and goal-oriented.

Children are only young once. If they have hours of homework in grade one they are in the wrong school. If they have three hours of homework in high school that is perfectly fine. I strongly believe that we should change our education system. Kids under the age of 15 should be in classes for no more than 4 hours per day. The remainder of the time should be spent involved in sports, outdoor activities, music, art, and independent study. The school should be a place where leaders are cultivated and supported, definitely not what we call school today.

I know I reminisce and have times where I wish I would have had a better education, more access to elite sports programming, or more money to pursue what I wanted. However, one of the most important lessons I learned is that it is not the education from books that is important, but the learning from interacting with others, playing sports, being a leader in activities, and using my imagination that made me who I am today.

What a great school looks like

I want a school for my children that listens to parents, a school that provides more than I expect. I want a school that can manage my daughter's allergies, educate her, teach her sports at a high level, allow her to learn languages, learn about the human body, nutrition, the environment, and teach her wellness and stress management strategies from grade 1. I want a school that will guide my daughter to take university programming, that will give her a successful career in nursing, medicine, or dentistry. I want my school to teach my children martial arts, skiing, skating, hiking, and camping. I want my children to feel safe.

So does this exist? Yes.

<u>BRAID Academy School of Excellence - BRAIDAcademy.com</u>

Since a great school that has the activities and learning that we suggest above doesn't exist, a group of medical doctors has teamed up to initiate a new international boarding school based out of Calgary, Canada - a location only 45 minutes from the Rocky Mountains. The school is named - BASE - Braid Academy School of Excellence. BRAID: 3 strands are stronger together than apart, the three strands being education, sport, and wellness.

The school will be a boarding school from grades six to twelve and day school from grades one to six. The school will run six days per week for seven weeks. Every seven weeks there will be a ten-day break for the entire school. This will allow for relaxation and rest to be therapeutic.

BASE is a stream specific school. It will not focus on teaching students about everything. That is not physically possible. Students cannot retain such vast information and be expected to apply it. It is here where this school differs. The Canadian curriculum will be taught in the school as a base, however a health sciences curriculum, based on the Canadian medical school model will be supplemented. Here students will learn about anatomy, physiology, nutrition, and the environment - all from grade one. This school will teach art and music - but it will not aspire to be a school that excels in these areas. Our goal is to educate well-rounded children that are given the ability and time to truly excel. This may be in the areas of environmental science, nursing, pharmacy, medicine, nutrition, golf, tennis, or outdoor pursuits.

The sports program will also be unique. We will teach children all the major sports - such as basketball, volleyball, and ice hockey, however our main focus will be outdoor sports such as hiking, mountain and road cycling, skiing - cross-country and downhill, canoeing and more. For those who desire there will be two elite sports programs that will include tennis and golf.

Our wellness program will be doctor-driven. All staff and students will receive quarterly medical checkups to assist in preventing disease by early detection. All staff and students with medical conditions will have focused care. Children with type 1 diabetes will have a safe environment to learn and play. This will be the first international boarding school that welcomes students with medical conditions. Having a school run by medical doctors will give parents a chance to breathe again and reduce stress. Parents will be comforted to know that the staff at the school, full time nurses, and full time doctors will be able to respond to any emergency their child may have.

If you're interested in becoming a part of the school, feel free to contact me through the website. We have plans to enrol the first class in August 2017.

What does it take to succeed?

To excel at sport, education, or wellness you need a vision, a goal and a plan on how to achieve it. It takes hours to perfect your craft. Studies show that to excel, one needs to spend over 10,000 hours to excel to a world-class level. Nadal, Federer, Rory McIlroy, Nelson Mendela, Barack Obama, Oprah Winfrey, doctors, successful musicians are examples of people who put in their 10,000 hours. Are you willing to do that?

Chapter 3 - Why Medical School - is it worth it?

Medical school and the opportunities it provides are phenomenal. I'm still amazed at how versatile, flexible, emotionally rewarding, recession-proof, and financially lucrative the profession it is. I have tried to compare medicine to almost all professions. The only profession that I believe is comparable and perhaps exceeds medicine is being a professional athlete like in the NHL/NFL/MBL, or be a musician like U2 or Jack Johnson. The reason I say this is sport and music at its best can provide a great standard of living doing something you love to do. BUT and it's a very large BUT - the chances of you being successful at these 2 endeavours are less than 0.01% or less. Being a successful entrepreneur is another job that people aspire to that can be equally as rewarding.

Why MD School?

Service

For most of you - medical school planning doesn't have to start at age 5. It can start at age 15, 17, or even 35. I want you to try to start as early as you can, but it's not "make or break" like sports are. In sports there is a certain age where you can not longer be competitive. Also medical school has advantages over sports and music as well. It provides a life-long career where you are providing people in need with care and support when they need it most. Patients trust you, your community trusts you, and your place in society is a special one. Medicine is a wonderful profession in this way.

Financial Stability

Doctors are amongst the top 3% of earners in North America. Family Doctors working a typical 40 hour week in Canada can earn between $200,000 to $650,000 per year, every year for the rest of their lives. Specialists can earn even more. Even athletes or musicians can't usually do that for their entire lives. It provides recession-proof, life-long access to an amazing quality of life. People will always need help with their health and will always need doctors. That's what we are here for. We get paid to help people get better. I have to admit that's pretty cool.

Personal Satisfaction

Medicine is also very rewarding to the spirit. If you have one - you will know what I'm talking about - if you don't - just go take a bathroom break and skip the next few lines. Everyday I have the opportunity to make someone's life a little easier by providing them with care, compassion, and a smile. If they leave the room feeling a little better than when they came in, or with a smile on their face, I feel better. When I feel better I have more energy to give to my children, my family, my patients, but most of all - myself. This leads me to the next point.

Being in control

Being your own boss is a huge sense of freedom. Not having anyone watching over you, counting the hours you have worked, checking your work all day, or hovering over you. I'm sad even writing this. This is most likely your life if you are not a business owner, a doctor, or homeless. Not having to answer to anyone is a powerful feeling. It's like being free to fly when you want. You don't have to ask for permission to take a break, or just leave if you're having a bad day. You're the boss and you're in charge of your schedule, how much money you make, and where you want to live.

Happiness

Sure people say money can't buy you happiness, but I disagree. Money can buy you the time, space, and the opportunity to be happy and provide happiness to others. This is what it does for me. If you wake up in the morning happy to go to work, knowing you will be able to provide for yourself and your family, leave a financial legacy, and provide a service to others - you will be happy. Ask any poor person if money would make them happier. Ask any person who was homeless and now successful – and there are many examples - they will tell you the same. Money provides opportunity for you to be happy. You don't have to take that opportunity but it is there.

Flexibility

In medicine, especially family medicine, you can work 3 days a week or 7 days a week. You can work for 3 months or 12 months. A friend of mine works 3 days a week and makes $240,000 per year as a Family Physician in Alberta. Not so bad? She is with her kids 4 days a week. Wow, that's tough. When she wants to go to Hawaii or California - she plans a couple of weeks in advance and is gone. All she needs is a few days notice and someone will cover her shifts. When she gets back from her trips she ramps it up for a few weeks to help pay the bills. This is the same for most physicians out there. They live a very good life. If they don't - they may have personal problems such as health issues affecting them or a loved one, otherwise they are just poor planners and don't know how to manage their money. Remember, medicine doesn't teach you how to run a business, and when you're done, you're running a business.

Relocation possibilities

Being a Canadian-trained doctor, I can work in any province in Canada and many states in the US without even doing any additional exams or tests. All I need to do is submit my documentation, move, and obtain my provincial license to practice medicine. That's pretty amazing. I could quit working In Calgary and move to Edmonton next weekend. Open up shop and start seeing patients in a matter of days. If I wanted to move to Halifax, I could. Palm Springs? No problem. I don't know many jobs that you can do that and still earn a fantastic living.

Education

I love to learn. I can never get enough material when I like something. I'm passionate about fitness and sport. I'm training my 3 and 6 year olds at Tennis at the moment and reading up on sports injuries, nutrition, and sports Psychology. I get to do this and get paid for it. All my learning translates to my patients and they get better care. Being a life-long learner is something you need if you want to go into medicine. Then again, if you don't like to learn- you are like a dead person. If you can't learn and accept change, you just have a pulse and are breathing - which frankly I think is worse and such a waste of this precious life. Come take a walk in the palliative care unit of a hospital with me, or see a patient who wishes she could shower without needing assistance. Maybe they'll spark some life back into you.

Respect and Advocacy

The day I got into medical school, everything changed. People respected me when I told them what I was doing, they wanted to know more. The banks were competing to give me a $200,000 credit line. After my medical school degree, when people ask me what I do, I'm humbled by the respect and trust people place in me just because of my profession. This is why I feel so many people ask me about how to get into medical school, and my recommendations. People feel that they trust doctors because of all the training we have been given, the hoops we have had to jump through, and what we do on a daily basis.

I don't think anyone is perfect, definitely not me, I make mistakes everyday. Big ones and small ones. We all do. But this "doctor status" gives me respect from others that I never felt before. It's like feeling you're part of an elite private club. Even billionaires respect the hard work that doctors do. One can easily earn the respect of even the most wealthy. My favourite part of having this respect is advocating for the less fortunate. Being able to go to bat for someone who may need medications, need some help at home, and to be able to advocate for community projects like a community playground. When I say, "Hello, I'm Dr. Kaler," people listen. Is this worth going to medical school for? No, but I think it is one of the perks that comes with the territory and it's important for me to be honest and tell you about everything I know.

In summary - medicine is one of the best professions I have come across. Not many professions can provide the characteristics I have mentioned.

Chapter 4 - For the Immigrant Parent and Child

Most immigrants I know work terribly hard. Many work two jobs. Others have had to go back to school in their 40's and 50's. You may wonder why have a separate chapter for immigrant parents? I am born to two immigrant parents and they wanted to help me accomplish my dream but had no clue how to do this. For those of you who are not born to immigrant parents, this section may not be as pertinent - but read on for interest.

When my parents heard I was interested in medicine, they wanted to help me. They asked their friends - both immigrant and Canadian-born — but no one offered to help. Even doctors they knew in the Indian community and Asian community didn't help. They said, "it's too hard" or "you can't afford it" or "my son had to go to Ireland". Another said, "my daughter had to go to the Caribbean." Constant negativity. No guidance.

I recently recognized some patterns relating to why these parents and cultures do this to each other. Most parents want what is best for their child and their family. Sometimes knowing that someone else may be more successful than you is seen as a threat. Threats are seen as a fear in the mind, and when fear sets in - watch out. Many people don't want others to know their secrets. They want to remain on top and don't want to share the podium. This frame of thinking is rampant in many immigrant families.

My parents didn't openly tell me they wanted me to become a doctor. That was good. They encouraged me to go to school and become a professional in the hopes that I would have a stable career and be able to support my family. This was ingrained in my mind from a young age. I believe there is nothing wrong with this. Being a professional usually means job stability, not having to work a laborious job when one ages and the body physically can't take it. Like I mentioned before, many immigrant parents were very educated in their country of origin, for example, working as doctors, lawyers or in businessmen. Since their education is not recognized in Canada, they are forced to work labour-intensive jobs. Many had no intention of doing this when they immigrated to Canada, but they did what was necessary at the time and became entangled in this way of living and couldn't escape.

So, parents, you don't need to do anything special. There is no need to buy presents for your kid's teachers. You don't have to make buddy-buddy with doctors in your community. All you have to do is read this book and develop a plan. Then, work hard to execute it. I have laid out the plan in the book. Don't think this book is any excuse for hard work. It's not. But now you can create a plan and your hard earned money will be spent in the right way. I know that most of you immigrant parents would happily spend your life savings on your children. This is partly why I have written this chapter for you. I want you to spend your hard earned money wisely, NOT WASTE IT. But to do this you need a dream, a guide, a plan, and faith in yourself.

DIAMOND - To be Successful you Need a Dream, a Guide, a Plan, and Faith in Yourself.

The two major places you can waste your money as a parent are private schools (not all but most), and going to large universities for pre-professional programs. Please read this carefully. Whenever you spend money on your children, think to yourself:

- "Is it worth it?"
- "What am I getting for my money?"
- "Will this help my child be successful?"
- "What is the proof?"

If you can answer three of the four questions with a "yes" - then you know you are on the right track. I encourage you to read my chapter on private schools, to better understand my view of what makes a good private school, and a good university. To remind you - I went to a public school and did not feel like it gave me the tools to succeed in university. However, many private schools that I have visited also don't meet the criteria of what I'm looking for. I went to a large university and initially did very poorly because of a variety of factors. One of those factors was going to a large school. Going to a small college or university will give you the ability to learn more from the teachers, be more competitive like I mentioned earlier in the book.

If you are the child of an immigrant...

Please take what I'm about to say with a grain of salt. Most parents mean well. They don't want you to have a life like theirs - they want yours to be better. This is why so many parents push and encourage their children. Don't let it turn you off. Don't let it turn you away from your path. The problem with most pushy parents is that many of them are so tired, angry, lonely, and disappointed with their own life - that they have no one to take this out on except for you. Immigrant parents will rarely, if ever, show this side or open up in fear of embarrassment from their community. This is not right and future generations will hopefully change this, but for now we have to work with what we've got.

I'm here to help you plan most of these things out. Sometimes, needs and wants don't always align and that is for many reasons, which I won't go into here. Having a professional degree as a "backup" is a great way to plan your future. If you're going to work hard and do a degree anyway - why not have one that pays you well? We could use nursing as an example. Compare the four-year biology degree to a four-year nursing degree. Both have the same amount of tuition. You will have a difficult time getting a job with a bachelors degree in biology, while nursing positions are almost always available and pay between $60,000 to $100,000 per year. Trust me, money matters. When you're done school and need to pay for rent, insurance, food, car, sports, clothes, your iPhone - your salary will matter.

What can you do? Work hard, be a warrior, be relentless, don't stop, don't give up. Put the tips from this book into ACTION. Medical school and professional schools are very competitive. You must be willing to give 200% to get in. You need to know there was no stone left unturned and that you did all you could. This will eventually be met with rewards. This feeling is one that I will never be able to explain to you. I want you to experience it yourself.

Another benefit you will see is when you gain admission to a professional program or complete it, your parents will change. It is as if a pressure and burden has been lifted from them and you can physically see it. They feel like their job is done. Also when your parents get older you will be able to provide for them, afford nursing care, and other medical expenses. You may be able to buy them a condo, send them on that trip they never took, or bring their family here to visit them. All this will cost money and if you're in a professional position you will be able to support them. Best of all, you will feel confident in your ability to do this. This is a feeling that is also extremely gratifying.

So to parents - work hard, save money, try to obtain help from people who are genuinely interested in helping you out. Please be nice to your kids and do push them - just not too much. You should know when you have gone too far and apologize for that. However, you do need to push, as many young people do need a kick-start and encouragement. I promise you when you're done achieving your goals you will be thankful you worked hard.

DIAMOND - No one ever regretted working hard for something when they accomplished their goal. They only regretted it if they gave up. Never give up.

Chapter 5 - Private Schools vs Public vs Home Schooling

I know - how did I even think to put home-schooling into the equation? That is outrageous right? Or is it? We are a family of two doctor parents and 2 young girls ages 3 and 6. We researched many of the private, public, and boarding schools in Canada, the US, and Europe. What did we decide? Home schooling. Why? Because there just wasn't a school that fit our needs. No we are not environmentalists that live in a tent and don't immunize their kids. Far from it. I'm a tiger dad who wants the best for my children and is going to do anything to give it to them. Again, as I said in the earlier chapters - I would be willing to pay any price to have my children in a school that had what I was looking for, but I'm also not willing to pay $10.00 to send my child to a school that doesn't. It's just the way I work.

Yes, one of us had to stay at home and take a pay cut, but we also consider this as an investment we will not regret. This is not an option for many of you, and since Braid Academy is not yet built, your options are home schooling or public schooling. I don't think it is worth spending your money on private schools in Canada or the US - yet. If something changes I will update this chapter in a further edition of this book, or on my website. Remember this is not about hockey, rugby, being well rounded. I'm looking for a school that is intensely laser focused on stream specific education like health professions, outdoor pursuits, and wellness. We need to teach our kids how to be great at a few things, and okay at the rest.

Private schools - Liars and cheaters.

Whats wrong with private schools?

1. Private schools label themselves as Not-for-Profit/Charities. YES! A total of 98% of private schools label themselves as Not-for-Profit/Charities. They charge parents $25,000 to $50,000 each year, have a yearly revenue of $15 to 50 million (depending on tuition fees and the number of students) and they pay no federal/provincial/state tax! Their CEOs can make $500,000 per year (and sometimes double that). To make things worse, they then ask the provinces for funding and get between $6000 to $8000 per student per year from the government because of their charity status. So, in addition to the $50,000 they are collecting from you, they are getting another $7000 from your province. Sound morally wrong? I think so. I believe public money is for people who can't afford education - not for private schools. They shouldn't get $1.00 from our public system.

2. Jack of all - Master of none. This was one of my fathers favourite sayings. He used to encourage me to be great at something, rather than good at a lot of things. At open-house sessions private school students and parents are told about the 50 clubs they have, the 75 sports programs, and the 10 languages they offer. Their admission rates to universities are 99.8%, blah, blah, blah. This is mostly a marketing scheme to get parents to feel they are inadequate if they don't send their children to one of their schools. Sadly it works. If you dig deeper, you find out that they may have many clubs, sports programs, and high admission to universities - but so many of these schools excel at very little. They have no detailed vision and goals for their school.

Few of them publish their admissions statistics to professional programs. Ask them to prove how many doctors they produce? If they give you a number, ask for proof. Getting into university is easy. Getting into medical school or professional programs is hard. Do you want your kid to be able to be good at everything and great at little? Then private school maybe for you. If your school doesn't have a focus and isn't stream specific, it's a waste of your money - choose a public school instead. It will do the same job at 1% of the cost.

3. <u>All show and no action.</u> Many parents want to tell others (and their ego) that their child goes to "Hollywood Charter" or "A+ Academy" (these don't exist but the names of some of these private schools today are so ridiculous). However, this can't be the main reason for you spending tons of money on these schools. I understand status is important, but you need to be critical and make sure the school you choose is providing you with what your family needs and provides your children with a unique experience that will help them be successful in life.

4. <u>Lame Outdoor programming</u> - As a physician and outdoor enthusiast, this was a huge reason for us to home school our kids. Research shows that nature has protective and preventative healing properties. Trees, for example, increase the levels of human NK cells (cancer fighting immune cells) when we walk or sit in the forest. So why doesn't the public/private school system address this? Because they don't care. The public system is so mismanaged and short of money that they are trying to survive with ever increasing class sizes. Private schools are all about numbers of students and revenue generated. They mostly want your

money. In Switzerland, where schools cost an average of $100,000 per year, a school representative mentioned to me that the children do hikes once a semester. Their web-site labeled them as "the best outdoor school in Switzer-land." In Canada and the US, the same problem exists. Parents are given a false sense of what their children will do once they attend. In addition, parents have to pay extra if their children want to go hiking, skiing, or on a camping trip. Why is this not included in the $50,000 to $140,000 tuition fees? Why can't kids go on a hike, ski, canoe trip, skating every week with the school?

5. Private schools are full of bureaucracy - students and fami-lies have very little input unless they donate money. One of my best friend's daughters went to a boarding school on Vancouver Island and she explained to me how the staff would rarely take parent and student opinion into account. Even their student leaders and council were picked by the staff with no impact of the student body vote. The apathy of the student body was apparent. Aren't these schools ad-vertising leadership skills and critical thinking? Waitlists are another hurdle to overcome. Schools will state there is a 2 year waitlist to be enrolled, however if you donate $5000 to the school you will have an acceptance letter in your mailbox in a few weeks. In another circumstance a fake wait list was made to enhance optics of the school and the difficulty to get in.

6. Private schools have a double standard for discipline. If students are expelled for having drugs such as cocaine or marijuana, many of them return the following year because their parents donated to the school. Is that okay? Other students with offences, like being caught drinking alcohol,

are expelled and never allowed to come back because their parents didn't pay to get their child back.

DIAMOND - *There is no private or boarding school that meets my standards. So why should you waste your hard earned money?*

Public schools - modern daycare.

Today public schools are a sad reflection of our society. Many of them try to do the best they can, but they are loaded with top end bureaucracy that won't let them make the changes necessary at a grass roots level. States and provinces make blanket changes and try to implement this to all schools across cities and rural settings, when the dynamics are extremely different depending on each district.

Most school hours are arranged around the work day. This was to help parents who need to be at work. To allow them to drop their kids off at school and then pick them up after work. They then feed our children garbage, if they feed them at all. Parents who stay up late to cook healthy meals eventually burn out or resort to hiring help if they can afford it. Nowadays, schools in my home province charge parents a "lunch fee" if they want their children to be supervised during the lunch break. Things are only getting worse with this system.

Outdoor time and physical activity - public schools have cut back and reduced physical activity and outdoor time. Our children are more obese than ever and have more chronic disease than ever. Is classroom time more important than their physical health? When did the shift occur? Why? As a society we have to ask what we are doing to help the epidemic of chronic diseases in young people. Is it okay to have type 2 diabetes in a 8 year old? Or the exponential increase of obesity in our youth? Is it okay to feed our children fries, hotdogs, pasta, and pizza every day? I'm embarrassed for our society at how far we have let things go. How little we revolt and stand up for our children, education, our health, and our healthcare.

DIAMOND - *If we don't take care of our children now, why should they take care of us when we're older?*

Many people have become apathetic today, including teachers, school boards, and communities. Many feel they can't influence change. Many people say - "we need a leader", "someone else needs to do it", "why doesn't the government do something", "things are so bad". Teachers don't raise their voices and revolt because the ones that did before them got nowhere, parents don't get upset and demand change because they are too tired and stressed. Do you feel the apathy? We can not just give up because the people before us were unsuccessful. We need to push ahead, make change, fight for change. The elected officials work for us, not the other way around. We need to demand a different way - and the only way to do this is to get together and get behind an initiative you believe in. This is what I have decided to do.

Homeschooling - the new trend. Home schooling is a great option for parents who want to give their children a variety of experiences: travelling, learning outdoors, going ahead and skipping a few grades, taking the pressure off and having no exams until high-school (yes this is true!). Sport-involved parents wanting their children to play tennis, hockey, baseball, may find homeschooling a life saver. They can train their kids when they are most alert and work around their practice and training schedules to educate them. This works well for the musically inclined family as well.

There are many disadvantages to home schooling as well. Parents who don't like to teach, are not organized, and don't have the skill set to plan can cause more harm to a child's learning. Financially, it may be difficult to home school in a family that depends on two incomes. Parents need to be uber-motivated and search out programming for their kids so that they can interact and socialize.

Why doesn't anyone build a school that solves these prob-lems?

That is exactly the question I have had for the past decade. I have decided to address this by building a school that meets all the criteria I demand from an educational institution. A group of medical doctors have decided to build BRAID Acad-emy. A school that will have NO support from the public sys-tem.

The school will be stream specific focused on: education - primarily health sciences/environmental education, Sports - outdoor education along with tennis and golf, and most im-portantly, Wellness - a program that has onsite full-time doc-tors with quarterly health assessments and an allergy friendly nutrition program that professional athletes receive. If you're interested visit www.BRAIDAcademy.com

Chapter 6 - Choosing an Undergraduate Degree

This is another "Diamond" chapter that is important. Even if you are not interested in medicine or health professions you should read this chapter. Give it to your friends. If you can't afford to buy them a copy, photocopy this chapter and give it to them - I give you permission.

DIAMOND - Do an undergraduate degree that gives you a well paying job at the end of it. Period.

You can question what I'm saying, but I ask you to be open minded. Please read, listen, evaluate, and then go ahead and make the necessary changes to give you the best chance of employment and stability for you and your family. If you are a high school student, you're in the best position right now. You can choose from any of the following professional programs I list below. Now to those students that are saying, "Hmm... I want to do a degree in chemistry, or biochemistry, or marine biology," stop reading this book and throw it out. This book is about health professions and medical school. If you want to get into medical school, dentistry, or a health professions program - you will gain from listening to my advice. Remember your decisions are very important. Please take them seriously. This is your life and there is a lot on the line.

Let me be very clear. Most interested in medicine or dentistry,should plan to do an undergraduate degree that can provide you with a sustainable income if you don't get into medical school. The only exception to this rule is if you're parents are filthy rich - like Kevin-O'Leary-rich. Then, who gives a crap? Do what you want. If you don't get into medical school you will have a great backup. For those of us that don't have that option to rely on - read on.

Doing a degree in nursing, for example, will provide you with an average salary between $60,000 to $90,000 per year (in some locations much more)- working 4 to 5 days a week, with full health benefits, and vacation time. All this for completing a 4 year program. If you did what I did - get a degree in Chemistry - you can work at a coffee shop making $18,000 per year, working 5 to 7 days a week, have no benefits, and to 3 weeks vacation per year if you're lucky. I spent $17,000 on my undergrad degree, and so does a nursing student. Who made the better decision? The nurse.

Other great examples - Pharmacy, Education, Engineering, Physiotherapy, Nutrition, and Social work. All these will provide you with a stable income as soon as you're done if you don't get into medical school. Remember the average applicant applies a total of 2.8 times in Canada before they get in. Go work and make some money during this time off. It shows maturity and makes you unique. These are the best assets you have in your application. You can then use the money you're earning to pay your parents back, or pay your debt off. You can also use this money to study and fix what needs to be fixed in your application. Once you get in you will be able to use all this knowledge in medicine. Nurses in my class did amazing and many things came so easy to them. One of my respected nurse colleagues is preparing to be a general surgeon. A pharmacist in my class was the go-to person to ask about medications. The social worker in my medical school class was always the one to advocate for change. All these people got into medical school - get the point?

Grades Grades Grades

My only caveat to the undergraduate degrees I mentioned is Engineering. This is a very challenging degree where it will be tough to get an A average over 4 years. It will give you a job at the end of 4 years, but you may not get into medical school if you got low grades. I would rank this last on your list unless you're brilliant like some of the math guru friends I have. Just remember, if medicine is the goal, pace yourself. You're going to need all the energy you can get. Pick a degree that is "easier" and that you can do well at and maybe even enjoy. You are going to need to get a great GPA during your degree, so you need to work hard, but pick something that won't be as mentally exhausting. I tend to lean towards nursing, pharmacy, nutrition, social work, occupational therapy, physiotherapy, and education for this. They are all very respectable, stimulating jobs, relevant to medicine. I have a friend making $110,000/year as a teacher with 2 months off in the summer! Come on people!

List of best undergraduate degrees and Jobs

List of Best Undergraduate degrees and Jobs *
Nursing
Pharmacy
Education
Physical Therapy
Occupational Therapy
Speech Language Pathology
Nutrition
Social Work
Police Force
Military
Engineering

* In no particular order

Let me summarize - do a degree that gives you a well paying job and apply to medical school. If you don't get in you will be making money while you re-apply. If you don't want to re-apply you will be making money! If you choose a non professional program you may be cleaning glassware in someone's lab making $11 per hour inhaling chemicals all day.

Remember you need a PhD in chemistry, biology, or other science to start making good money and get hired at a university as a professor. In today's economy this is not as easy as you think. Your job security in the academic world will depend on publications, research grants, and who you know. Then you're still walking on egg-shells to try to manoeuvre your way around to protect your job and you are definitely not the boss. This process to become a tenured professor at a university takes about 10 years on average. If you are getting worked up and are a researcher - put the book down and re-read the cover. This is about getting into health professional programs, not research programs. If you made mistakes and are doing research and screwed up your undergrad, consider quitting now (or completing the degree if you are nearing the end), and move in a direction that will help your application.

I have added smaller subsections on Nursing, Education, Dentistry, Nutrition, Pharmacy, and Social work below.

Nursing

Nursing is a 2 or 4 year program depending on what prov-ince/state you reside in or are planning on attending. Nurses can earn between $60,000 - $130,000 per year. This depends on the state/province you work in, your experience, and the job opportunity. Nursing also prepares you for medical school as you are working with patients daily. You also be-come fluent in medical jargon and learn numerous procedures during your program. If you don't get into medical school for a few years or you decide that nursing is where your heart lies, that's great because you have the financial stability to support your family.

Admissions Canadian Programs

I have listed just a few brief examples of some schools in Canada and their admissions information.

British Columbia

University of Northern British Columbia - UNBC

The UNBC program in Prince George offers a collaborative nursing program. The program is four years and you need to following courses to apply. Mathematics grade 11, Chemistry grade 11, and English grade 12 all with a minimum grade of 67% (C+), and Biology 12 with a minimum of 73% (B).

British Columbia Institute of Technology - BCIT

BCIT has an accelerated 3 year bachelors of science nursing program. The requirements are Chemistry - Grade 11, Math - Grade 11, English - 2 years at an english speaking school in an english speaking country. Then you require 18 university credits at a first year level including English, anatomy and physiology, psychology, and 2 elective courses (any courses you like at a first year university level.

ALBERTA

Mt. Royal University Nursing program

This is a four year program that you can take directly out of high school, or you can transfer in from other various pro-grams. You need to have the following high school courses. English with a minimum of 60%, Mathematics - minimum of

60%, Biology 30 - minimum of 50%, and either chemistry, physics, or science 30 again with a minimum of 50%. When I was reviewing this section I couldn't believe how low the requirements were. You can do this, and if you're grades weren't that good, you can always upgrade.

These are just a few examples of nursing schools you can choose to attend, there are numerous options. If you are interested in nursing as an option out of high school, or to transfer into nursing please go ahead and do some more research on the schools across the nation. Remember as you read through the book to choose a school that meets some of the "diamond criteria" I have listed. Small school, small class sizes, and in a province with the best admissions statistics for medical school.

Pharmacy

Pharmacy is also a four year program. It is slightly more difficult to get into that nursing, however if you put your mind, heart, and sweat into it, you can achieve it. Pharmacists can make anywhere from $65,000 to $500,000 and more depending on if you have your own pharmacy, work for someone, and how busy the pharmacy is. I have a pharmacist friend who makes $650,000 per year off of his single busy pharmacy.

The other benefits of pharmacy include the ability to know medications better than all your doctor colleagues, and your superiors in medicine. Most medical doctors only had a few days of pharmacology training versus the four years of a pharmacists. This will be a huge aid during your training and when you are done. I still consult pharmacists on a weekly basis for their advice. They are a great part of the team.

Nova Scotia

Dalhousie University Pharmacy Program

Pharmacy is again like medical school a provincially funded program. Many programs including pharmacy have spots reserved for candidates of their "home province" which you will learn more about throughout the book. Basically 90% of the spots are reserved for people from Nova Scotia, PEI, and New Brunswick.

You need to have done a complete year of university education with five courses in each semester - fall and winter. For those of you that don't understand this lingo - "fall semester" means September to December, and "winter semester" means January to April.

In that year you need to have taken the first year courses in Chemistry, Biology, Math, Statistics, social sciences, and English. All these need to be at 70% or above to be considered for admission. Now you don't have to take these courses at Dalhousie University but they must transfer as such. To find out if your courses transfer you just contact the admissions department of the school you would like to apply to and they will provide you with the details you need to provide.

Saskatchewan

University of Saskatchewan

The University of Saskatchewan offers a pharmacy program that is four years in length and it also requires university pre-requisites like Dalhousie and other pharmacy programs across Canada. Their current statistics for students applying from inside their province is 40% admissions rates for all qualified applicants, and a 20% admission rate for out of province students. Currently courses required are first year university courses in biology, chemistry, organic chemistry, english, humanities, and a course from sociology, philosophy, psychology, or native studies. A minimum of 70% average is required for applying to this program.

For admission 60% of the criteria is based on grades, 30% on a test of critical skills, and the personal profile counts for 10%.

Nutrition/Dietician

Another fantastic professional opportunity as a life long career or as an adjunct to applying to medicine. As with pharmacy and nursing, nutrition provides a wealth of information that can be applied to medical training, but most importantly to practise once medical training has ended. The epidemic of obesity and the poor nutrition of our citizens is a growing epidemic. Having a sound understanding of nutrition is a perfect in combination with medicine.

Dieticians have completed their nutrition degree along with a practicum and an examination that registers them as "registered dieticians". This qualifies them to practise as a dietician. An example of an excellent school in Nova Scotia that offers this program is the Mount Saint Vincent University Nutrition program.

This program is based in a small school, in a province that has excellent admission statistics for medicine, and has a lower cost of living and education than many other states and provinces. The nutrition program is four years in length at MSVU. An average dietician can make between $65,000 to $110,000 per year depending on the province and location of work. Again this profession is a unique one that will enhance an application to medicine.

Police / RCMP

I know this isn't a degree and why am I including it? Because if you chose to do a chemistry or biology degree and don't want to do more schooling - think about this as a viable option to gain experience, do some upgrading on your marks, and apply. Really? YES - this profession makes your application unique. Admission committees like unique remember!

Canadian cities have local and provincial law enforcement officers. Most cities in Canada such as Vancouver, Calgary, and Toronto have local (municipal) police officers that cover the jurisdiction of the city. Other areas such as communities outside of major centres will be covered by a regional RCMP detachment. The police force is a commendable position offering great pay, health benefits, and community respect. Some municipalities have various schedules of shift work. I have seen of schedules that have two day shifts and two night shifts followed by four days off, or two days shifts and two days off - three night shifts and five days off. If you can do shift work and like the adrenaline filled work of law enforcement it is an excellent profession that will provide you and your family with a stable financially viable position, but it can also be an excellent stepping stone to medicine. The main reason behind this again is the uniqueness of the application. Unique applications are those that catch the readers eye, that are different than the norm. A police officer applying to medical school is unique!

To become a police officer there are many different routes. The most common route is finishing some basic university/college schooling and then applying to the relevant enforcement agency. The RCMP for example does not require a undergraduate degree but allows if you have completed one you do not need to write their RCMP entrance exam. After this you need to pass a series of examinations such as an eye exam, physical health exam, questionnaire, interview, and security clearance. For municipalities an example of the Ottawa police service application, one must complete high school, be 18, and be of "good moral character and habits". Then there is a similar process to the application to become an RCMP officer.

If you are interested in this route then you should inquire at your local law enforcement agency or using the internet to help guide you. The average police officer in Ontario makes between $70,000 to $110,000 per year. Not bad for being able to apply directly out of high school.

Physiotherapy

Like the rest of the professional programs listed, physiotherapy is a rewarding career and can provide tremendous benefit to patients. In my residency program I had a colleague who was a physiotherapist in a previous occupation and was by far the best person to ask regarding joint or muscle related injuries. Since family medicine is 25-35% muscle and joint related concerns a physiotherapist has a tremendous advantage over someone who has a biochemistry degree.

Again the physiotherapist application is unique and that is what catches the eye of the admissions committee once you have met the grade point average. When it comes time to shine on the interview and final application the unique application will win most times if not always.

The masters in physiotherapy program in Manitoba requires a bachelors degree in any area of study, a minimum average of 3.25 or B+ average in the last 60 credits of university, and a 3.0 or B average in the pre-requisite courses that are required such as: Anatomy, physiology, biology, three courses in psychology, course in the elderly, statistics, and english. Once you are admitted you complete a two year program and receive a masters in physiotherapy. Instead of doing a masters in chemistry which will provide you with little relevant learning for medicine and little income, a masters degree in physiotherapy can provide you with a well paying job with excellent benefits and the chance to be your own boss if you so desire. Some physiotherapists in vancouver make well over $100,000 / year. The main reason for this high salary is that many health care plans cover physiotherapy as an insured service which means the patient does not pay out of pocket, which usually means more frequent visits and more money. Physiotherapists work in hospitals, family medicine clinics, or have their own practises.

Military

The military is an excellent option for those looking to obtain a medical degree. I have known five such individuals throughout my training that partook in this pathway. Ten years ago there were signing bonuses for doctors to join the military (sometimes as high as $200,000), but since the military has met its quota for doctors it has scraped this avenue and now focused on maintaining their present health care service by training medical students under the military officer training program (MOTP). Again like with the RCMP there are various routes to become a military officer in medical school. A high school student could join the military directly out of high school, and then pursue education at a university/college through the support of the military. In these cases the military usually pays the tuition and a salary to the student, providing that they work summers and other vacation at their local base. This is a very lucrative option as you are making a wage while studying with no expenses on tuition fees and books. When done an undergraduate degree as a military officer one can apply to medical schools that have MOTP seats. These are medical schools that have seats reserved for MOTP applicants. Once admitted the student will have their tuition paid for ($16,000 to $25,000/year) books, supplies, and other fees covered. In addition they will collect their officer salary which in the case of one of my friends was well over $65,000 per year. Not a bad way to go through medical school.

At the end of your training you must provide a minimum return of service of five years. This may change in the future but at the writing of this edition of the book this is the norm.

If you're interested in this option, learn more by researching the military websites and talk to recruitment officials about various positions in the military and going to school as a military officer. This is also a unique way to gain admission to medical school. A military officer is definitely a unique applicant.

Chapter 7 - Choosing your state or province of study

Another DIAMOND Chapter here - don't let it slip. These 2 chapters are crucial here so read and re-read until you understand.

DIAMOND - Do your undergraduate degree in a province with the best admissions statistics.

Okay so this is a taboo topic and many people get queasy thinking about it. I talk sometimes about having to break the rules, having to do whatever it takes to achieve your dream. This is the chapter that is most relevant. I don't think this is breaking the rules at all - I just think it's breaking your connection with home. It's getting you to wake up and see if you have what it takes, and for you to find out how bad you want to get in to these health profession programs.

I'm going to use Canada as an example, but the US is very similar and you should utilize a very similar strategy if you are a US student.

Spend a few days researching only statistics. Look at all the admissions websites for schools across Canada. See their admissions rates for "in province" (IP) students. I talk about this in more detail in Chapter 6. For example, UBC has a success rate of 16% for "In Province"(IP) students, compare this to Saskatchewan with an over"50%" IP admission rate in 2015. Just for your knowledge in Saskatchewan there were only 173 applications from Saskatchewan residents for 88 spots. Those are some amazing odds. Almost everyone who was a Saskatchewan resident received an interview. What province is the one you want to move to and apply to? Saskatchewan. In the past ten years the best provinces to do you undergraduate degree and the best IP admissions stats for medical school are listed below.

If you are an "Out of Province" (OOP) student the statistics are even worse. At UBC in 2015 only 27 people that were OOP were admitted from 737 applications, that's a success rate of 3%. Hopefully you are starting to see that finding a province where you have the best chance of admission is a good place to settle down, and who knows you may fall in love with the place and never leave.

Best admissions statistics to MD school in Canada

Provinces with Best IP admission rate	Rate
Saskatchewan (1) - U of S	51%
New Brunswick** (1) Dal NB	36%
Manitoba (1) - U of M	29%
New Foundland (1) U of NFLD	29%
Nova Scotia (1) - Dalhousie	21%

** NB is a Dalhousie Satellite campus but students admitted for IP seats are NB students.

A good plan of attack for admissions to medical school would be to move to a province with the best IP stats after grade 12 or even during high school if your parents are willing to move with you. Apply to all these IP places and rank them with the ones you would most likely want to live in. If you already live in one of these places - DON'T MOVE. I had to convince one of my physician colleagues who asked for my guidance to keep his daughter in Nova Scotia. He was thinking of sending her to another province. Now his daughter just started medical school at Dalhousie - ON HER FIRST TRY! Not even one rejection letter. That makes my heart smile.

Once you decide on a province and move there for your undergraduate degree you will have to decide which degree you will do. That could be nursing, pharmacy, social work, or the military officer training program, or one of the other choices I mention previously. Then at the end of your third year, you will apply to medical school if you have solid grades, and have your MCAT which you will also have to have written prior to the beginning of fourth year as you need your score to apply. Of course you could do your MCAT during the school year but you have that much time to study on the side of your regular academics you're either not the smartest cookie, or you are so smart that you don't need this book.

Make sure you do your medical school pre-requisites if they are not included in your degree program. You may have to do these in the summer or through distance education. This may be beneficial or detrimental depending on the school you apply to. Some schools don't count your summer school grades in your GPA because they think it is an easier course load - I think this is ridiculous - but hey, welcome to universities trying to find more ways to make it harder for you. However, on the flip-side, if your grades were poor in those pre-requisites then you'll be thankful that the grades don't count - but you got the checkmark on your application for completing the pre-requisites. Not all schools are like this - but I'm going to leave this to you to look into this topic as information changes yearly and can be found on the admissions websites of all the schools.

How to decide between provinces? Don't get too picky. Now if you live in Nova Scotia and the "IP" admission stats are worse than in Saskatchewan by a few points - don't move. You are already in a great province - unless you really want to move to try something new.

Chapter 8 - Statistics - you're not going to like it

Getting into medical school is hard. On average there are 28,000 applications each year in Canada alone. Of those over 28,000 applications only around 2,200 are accepted. That's a 10% admission rate and that seems pretty good to me. I know, I'm an optimist.

However, the numbers are worse than they appear. The rates vary by province. This is because some provinces like Ontario, British Columbia, and Alberta have a disproportionately higher number of applications compared to Saskatchewan, Manitoba, Quebec, New Brunswick, Nova Scotia, and Newfoundland. Some provinces like British Columbia may have nearly 3000 applications for less than 300 spots. Ontario's statistics are even lower at some medical schools. However as I mentioned above - Saskatchewan has an over 50% admission rate. One of my diamonds is to apply to a school that has a better rate of admission, and to gain residency in that province. Hey why not consider living there after you're done medical school too?

DIAMOND - Live, work, go to school, in a province with the best admission statistics.

Here is why. In Canada, education is not a national jurisdiction; it is provincial. So the provinces allocate how much money will go to what schools. Basically, medical school is largely funded by the provinces. I know even though tuition is nearing $20,000 at most institutions you wonder how much provinces are pitching in. It is estimated that the total cost to educate a single medical student is between $85,000 to $100,000.

If the provinces are funding these medical schools, then they want to fund residents of that province. The same happens in the US. If you are a resident of a state you can apply for 95-98% of the seats reserved for "residents of that province". If you are not a resident of that province you can apply for the remaining 2-5% of seats. Let us use the BC example: if you are applying to BC and there are 300 seats available - 95% of the seats are reserved for residents of BC or 285 seats. The remaining 15 seats are reserved for "OOP students" or Out Of Province students.

Now here is where the math comes into play. If you're from BC and there are 3000 applications in total for those 300 seats. You need to know how many of those 3000 applications were from residents of BC and how many were from out of province students. If there are only 1500 applications from BC applicants then the rate of admission for a BC resident to medical school in BC is 285/1500 = 19%. But if you're from Alberta and really want to go to Vancouver to live it up for medical school, you will have a tougher time. If we were to use the same example if there are 3000 applications to UBC medicine and 1500 are from residents of BC - that leaves 1500 for out of province students. Remember we said earlier that only 15 seats were reserved for out of province students. Now that means that 1500 people are competing for 15 spots at UBC - that give an out of province applicant a chance of admission of : 15/1500=1%.

I hope you are starting to see how this game is played and how confusing it can be. Don't worry, you have this book and the data below to help you understand this information better. Basically, you shouldn't be applying as an out of province student unless you are darn sure you are one of those students who has an A+ (4.0) GPA, saved kids in Rwanda, and won 2 gold medals in the 2010 olympics in Vancouver. Otherwise, you're wasting your money and time. Applications take lots of time. Save your money.

There are a total of 17 medical schools in Canada and the table below gives you some statistics. Don't just browse the numbers - pay attention, see if you find a pattern. You should.

I did not include the french speaking schools in the chart below because I don't feel that most of the applicants reading this book are thinking of going to a french school for medical school and then planning on staying in Quebec to practise medicine. If you're one of those applicants, sorry that I don't have statistics for you.

Next you will see that there are over 28,800 applications for medical school in 2015. There were only 2258 spots, which leaves an acceptance rate of 7.8%. Now that may sound good to you but don't forget that is 28,800 students with average GPA of A or 3.7/4.0. That is a lot of SMART people competing for those spots. I hope you can start to see why planning is so important.

Admissions statistics of Canadian medical schools 2015

MD school	Applicants Total	IP Accept	OOP Accept	Total Seats
Dalhousie	1183	21%	1.5%	110
Memorial	700	21.4%	1.4%	80
McGill	2602	10.8%	1.2%	279
Ottawa	4299	NA	NA	164
Toronto	3488	10.6%	0.07%	260
McMaster	5271	9.7%	0.03%	205
Western	2372	9.8%	0.9%	171
Queens	NA	NA	NA	106
North Ontario*	2130	19.7%	0.1%	64
Manitoba	971	29.4%	4.1%	112
Saskatchewan	694	50.8%	2.3%	100
Calgary	1402	12.4%	4.5%	157
Alberta	1441	11.6	5.3%	162
UBC	2322	17.6%	2.0%	288
Total	28875			2258

* From Northern Ontario
IP - In province applicants
OOP - Out of Province applicants.

Chapter 9 Medical School Admissions an overview of the process.

To understand how medical schools work, we need to look at the process.

The first step is to have the pre-requisite courses, degree, or other criteria that the medical school requires in order to apply. For some it will be a degree, for others it will be specific courses like biology, chemistry, etc. These pre-requisites are easily found on on every medical school website. Trust me, they are not hard to find when you google something like "dalhousie medicine - admission requirements". Why is it not hard to find - because the administrative staff don't want to answer 5000 more calls about the same questions like -"yes you need biochemistry and no your chocolate making class won't count as a pre-requisite".

Once you have these standard criteria you can apply.

DIAMOND - Every school has different admission criteria - MAKE SURE you know the criteria well in advance of applying so you can obtain the necessary requirements.

Here is the process in its entirety as an example.

1. Finish High school
        - June 2016

2. Go to college/university start Nursing Degree
        - September 2016

3. Write your MCAT in the year prior to applying
   -Summer of 2019 - third year.

4. Apply to MD schools of choice in 3rd year,
   - July 2019 for Starting August 2020

5. Application reviewed - based on grades, volunteering, extra-curricular activities, essay, references
   - Sep-Dec 2019

6. Applications ranked - from 1-2500

7. Top 600 interviewed - yes if you are number 601 you don't get an interview.
   - Usually in February 2020

8. Interviews done on site - mostly in a multiple mini-interview like format.

9. Interview score and Application score combined

10. 600 spots ranked 1-600

11. Individuals ranked 1-250 are accepted
    - usually April 2020

12. Individuals 250-275 (or another number) are waitlisted meaning if some people who got into multiple places turn their spot down at one school it opens up to a waitlisted spot.

13. You graduate from your undergraduate degree.

- May 2020.

14. You start medical school
    - August 2020.

15. Medical school is 4 years (most schools)
    - finish May 2024.

16. Residency training in Family medicine is 2 years, all
    other specialities usually 5 years.
    - Start July 2024, finish July 2026 / 2029

Total years from high school - if all goes right to become family doctor - 10 years. To become a specialist such as an Obstetrician or Surgeon it will take 13 years minimum.

So if you are going to invest 10 to13 years in your future, do you think you should have a guide? Just think, it took me 18 years to do what I hope takes you 10. Please listen and take control of your life. You can thank me later when you get in.

Does this seem to long? You have to ask yourself two questions. One - am I willing to put that kind of effort in, day after day, for years? If not - stop now and think that this $50.00 book saved you 10 to 15 years, and over $150,000. If you are ready and still not going to back down - you're someone with a lot of grit.

If you chose to go for it - don't worry. Remember, you could be doing something that you hate in 10 years as well, you might as well do something that you love. It is a long time, but time will fly and the hardest part is getting into medical school. Once you get in to medical school in Canada the programs are fantastic and will help get you through - unless you want to throw it away like a guy in my class who didn't show up to class or finish anything on time. The school tried to kick him out multiple times and he was held back and had to re-do some training but he still finished. But the norm is that once you get in, there is a very, very high success rate. They want you to finish. Residency is nothing like medical school admissions. It's much easier. If you want to do Plastic Surgery and are competing with a larger applicant pool then it will be tougher but not as hard as getting into medical school.

"You can work hard to do what you love now, or you can live easy and relax now and hate what you have to do for the rest of your life. You choose."

~N.Kaler

Chapter 10 - Extra - Curricular Experiences.

This is a word that you will most definitely get tired of hearing. It's also another topic to NOT ask you friends about. So many people will give you varying information on it and tell you that they did this or that - and then you're going to walk away with your tail between your legs because you didn't do what they did. Who cares! You're not the same as them. I'm going to help you develop a clear and well laid-out plan on how to approach the extra-curricular section on your application.

So what are extra-curricular activities/experiences? This is everything that you have done in your life not relating to academics. This includes volunteering, sports you have been involved in, and involvement in the arts or music. I will discuss each of these below and then give you my recommendation on each.

Before I get into the details and some examples, I want you to remember that this is EXTRA-CURRICULAR experiences - not CURRICULAR. The reason I am emphasizing this is that many students spend a majority of their time focusing on this as the main way to get themselves in. They talk about all the time. "Where should I volunteer this year? Maybe at the hospital like the other 20,000 pre-medical students volunteering there?" How unique... Your main focus must be your academics. You need to do well in your courses or no one will even get to read your extracurricular activities. How do I know? I made that mistake.

I volunteered in Aboriginal communities, was an International resident advisor, volunteered with the elderly, volunteered at the hospital, was president of my university ski club, volunteered at international ski races and other sporting events, then competed in sporting events all over the world, etc...

I don't want you to fall into the same trap that I did. School isn't always fun, studying isn't always fun. You're extra-curricular activities are usually fun. If they're not - then you're boring and lame. Stop doing things in you're spare time that aren't fun. My problem is that the more I did my extra-curricular activities the more I enjoyed them and it became an escape from academics. Not enough to make my grades suffer tremendously. However, my grades did suffer because I was spending time away from school and studying. I didn't see this coming. So make sure you do extra-curricular activities, but make sure they are fewer than 10 hours a week.

Okay, if you're a pro-athlete, play university sports, or are a musician you will need to train more - and that will take time from studying. It's your decision to make. Go for it if you're like one of my favourite classmates who had a near photographic memory, played on the varsity basketball team before AND during medical school, and then won all of the academic awards from our class. She was a superstar and dammit I wish I was like her sometimes, but I'm not. I'm me. You should think like that too. If things take work for you to do well, then you are going to need time to focus on those things - and studying will have to be one of them.

Extra-curricular activities are important to maintain some type of balance in your life so you don't burn out. This is why it is essential to pick something that you love to do. Something that will help relax you and give you a mental break from your studying and worrying. Exercise is a great activity to do and if you do an intramural sport, or endeavour to train for a cycling race that's great because you now are doing something that makes you feel better, and you can put it on your resume. Now that is efficiency.

This is all shown to help you live a full life that medical school committees love to see - a WELL-ROUNDED PERSON. I don't know if I completely believe in this idea, however it's a "key word" you're just going to have to accept and learn to conform to. That's what they want. Although this is important remember your grades are #1. If you have those then you're fine. The actual statement should be medical schools want you to have great grades and THEN be a well-rounded person.

DIAMOND - Use your extra-curricular activities to do sports or arts experiences that help provide you with an outlet from your daily grind.

Another important concept that I want to drill into your mind is the concept of being UNIQUE. You need to be unique, and if you're not unique then you're going to have a tough time convincing the application committee and then the interview committee to let you into medical school. There are just so many applicants nowadays and if you're story isn't interesting, you're not going to get in. You need to have something unique about your application and this is a great way to do that. Use this - NOT as a means to get in - but as a means to find yourself.

An example of being unique is someone who worked as a truck driver for 3 years doing long haul transport and then decided to go to medicine. Another unique example is an individual who worked as a pilot for five years and then felt medicine was a passion she wanted to explore. Some other examples? Nursing, Physiotherapy, Pharmacy, Engineering, Law, Teaching, Athlete, Welder, Construction worker, etc. Unique = Different.

In addition to being unique you need to learn how to tell your story. Humans are story tellers. Much of what we learn is based on stories from books and people passing information along. So if we are story tellers at our core, imagine the reviewers as people listening to a story. Make your story INTERESTING. If you don't think it is interesting, they surely won't. Sit back and think about your story, and how you need to word it so that you sound interesting because you are! If you don't think you're interesting then we have another slew of problems we need to address.

Examples of extra-curricular / unique activities

Volunteering

Local homeless shelter, salvation army, seniors home, palliative care, sports events - marathon running race, breast cancer walk, ski races, para-olympic events, music events, arts events. There are always 5-10 activities occurring in your city or surrounding area every week - look into these events and contact the organizer. Just make sure it is unique.

Sports

You can think of any sport you like here, just try to be a part of a team. This helps you be able to talk about leadership skills, working with others, difficult situations and other situations that people that are part of a team encounter. Teamwork is another "key word" for you to focus on and sports can provide that. Soccer, hockey, volleyball, tennis, golf, sailing, hiking clubs, canoeing clubs, swimming, ultimate frisbee, horse riding, skiing are all excellent examples.

Arts/Music

If you're a musician at heart then make sure you showcase this as part of your story. Be involved in music events and displaying your craft. Play at local pubs and venues. Volunteer to play music at seniors homes, or at a local child care centre. Pick up your guitar and head downtown to a homeless shelter. It doesn't have to be something that is on a large scale. With these examples you can cover the arts and music components of your application along with the volunteering component. Best of all this makes your application UNIQUE!

I know a prominent medical doctor who plays music to this day. I frankly think he is better at his music than he is a doctor which is a huge compliment since he got doctor of the year last year. Music is an important part of his life and I encourage you to continue this passion if you are someone like this as well. Imagine if this doctor I talked about was interviewing you and you discussed music and how passionate you were about it. He would be excited to hear you talk about it and you would get an excellent review from him.

The arts is also a huge field that many people can continue to focus on. Not only can you focus on painting and visual art, there is the written arts as well. You can submit pieces to local magazines about your views or recent poems you have written. This now becomes something you talk about on your application as your extra-curricular activity but also as a publication you have. I've published humanities articles in national journals and it is something I'm proud of. You too can do this and it will only add to your uniqueness.

Jobs

I touch on this topic throughout the book because frankly people who have worked in their lives and have experienced what it is like to make money and have to take care of themselves, a family, or others receive my respect. The reason is they are usually more mature, team players, have more depth of character, and hardworking. Having a job before you apply to medical school is a huge asset in my mind.

This is why I have asked you to pick a professional program for your university training such as nursing, social work, or physiotherapy. If you don't get into medical school you can start working and your application is only getting better with age like a fine wine.

I don't want to go into details on jobs I think are unique since I do this in detail already. I'll let you dream something up. I haven't talked about business though and I think this would be a good time to talk about it. In between applications I decided to open my own business. I did this for a few years and still to this day continue this work on. Actually it is a major reason I'm writing this book. When I couldn't get into medical school I decided to open up a business for the 18,000 - 20,000 students that weren't getting into medical school. I decided that I needed to find a better way on how to coach these families so that they wouldn't fall into the same trap that I did. This is when i did all my research on medical schools in Canada and I assisted 6 people getting into medical school and nursing and I couldn't believe how successful I was. This business opportunity taught me about how to run a business, marketing, independence, interdependence, and hard work. Eventually I was so successful I decided to use my own advice and kept applying. Guess what - I got interviews and acceptance letters and now I'm a doctor. Still to this date I get thank you letters from families and students who have been successful on their applications and are practising medicine, nursing or other occupations. This makes my heart smile. I got tired of having to repeat the same thing over and over for everyone so I decided to write this book. Do you see how taking a chance on me and establishing a business now has come full circle? I'm now writing a book so that I can help thousands of more people like you.

DIAMOND - Make sure your application is unique and learn how to tell your story.

Chapter 11 - MCAT

The dreaded MCAT. MCAT stands for Medical College Admissions Test. There are only a handful of schools that do not require the MCAT in Canada: McMaster, Northern Ontario School of Medicine, and University of Ottawa. In Canada 95% of medical schools and nearly all schools in the USA require students to write the exam. The AAMC (Association of American Medical Colleges) mentions that 85,000 students write the exam every year, just to give you an idea of how many people are interested in becoming medical doctors in North America alone. This test is organized and implemented by the AAMC. You maybe wondering why an American test is being used at Canadian medical schools? I wondered the same thing, and still to this date wonder the utility of the test. To me it is still nothing more than a screening tool and another way for schools to rank people easily. I don't agree with it, but you will have to most likely sit the exam.

Now before you get too excited and say " I'm just going to apply there since I'll have a better chance" - press your brakes. Everyone thinks this and that is why these schools get an overwhelming amount of applications.

The MCAT is a standardized exam that is multiple choice that assesses problem solving, social science, biological sciences, physical sciences, problem solving, and critical thinking. In 2015 a new format of MCAT exam has been implemented. The four major sections that are tested and scored are:

1. Biological and biochemical foundations of living systems

2. Chemical and physical foundations of biological systems
3. Psychology, sociology, and biological foundations of behaviour
4. Critical analysis and reasoning skills.

The test is two hundred and thirty questions and you get a total of 6 hours and 15 minutes to write the exam. Each section has 53-59 questions and is 90-95 minutes long with a break in between each section. The total "seated time" is over 7.5 hours. The Chemistry section for example is 59 questions long and has an allowed time of 95 minutes. There are 10 passages each with an average of 4-6 questions per set. There are then independent questions that have no relevant passage associated with them.

The test costs around $305 and you can write it a maximum of three times per year, four times in two years, and a maximum of seven times in your life. A voided exam DOES count for one of your writings. Hopefully if you study like I suggest you won't have to write the test more than once. If you do though it is important for you to read the AAMC "MCAT essentials "guide for the details. The test is offered 20 or more times a year.

DIAMOND - Be patient and consistent with the MCAT studying - start early - finish strong. Write as many tests as you can.

A study plan for the MCAT is simple - yes simple. You just won't like the advice I have to give. You need to work hard consistently. You should give yourself twelve to sixteen weeks. The more the better. You should not be doing a stressful work placement, research project or take care of three kids while studying. You will need to dedicate 30 hours a week for the entire twelve to sixteen weeks if you want to do well. Think of this as your job. Most people work an average of 37-50 hours a week. If you want to be a doctor - you better be able to dedicate 30 hours a week. If not - quit now.

You should buy ten MCAT exams from AAMC- the people who write the exam, or get them from Amazon. Don't buy Kaplan or Princeton review books - they are just out there to make money. Just spend the money and give it to AAMC or people that have photocopies of those tests. Do two tests per week for five weeks and repeat for a total of ten weeks. Sit down in a quiet room where you will have no disruptions for six hours, with a timer, paper, pencil, and courage. If you can get the online exams like I did, that's even better as you'll be able to simulate an actual exam. Just make sure you will have access to the exam for at least 1 month so that you can mark it and re-do it later. Sit down write the exam, take the break they have scheduled. Pretend it is the real thing. Now MCAT has partnered with the Khan Academy which has more than 1100 videos and 3000 review questions for studying for the MCAT! All free! (khanacademy.org)

Once you have written the exam - do not mark it that day. Go home, watch a movie, call a friend, do something fun. TRUST me you are going to need this, and you deserve it. The next day - yes it should be the next day - mark your exam. Start to score your exam. This should take you two to three times longer than it took you to write your exam. Now it is your job to pick the exam apart and see the PATTERNS. Standardized exams are standardized because they are based on patterns. My suggestion is to take a section like the biological science section the morning after an exam and first see if you got the questions write for the first stem and set of questions. If you don't know what I'm talking about then you haven't written an MCAT or looked at an MCAT exam. These exams are based on a stem, which is a paragraph of background information, followed by a series of questions. Once you have marked your first set of questions go back and slowly read thr the stem and see if any of the text would have helped you answer the questions. Highlight or underline these sections. Then the next step is to look up what you understood and didn't understand in the stem. Now go to google, wikipedia, other resources to better understand these words or concepts. Once you understand these concepts move onto the questions. Look at each question and see if the question was answered in the stem. Many of them are! No I'm not kidding. If you READ the question well you can probably get the answer just by looking at the stem and the question before even looking at the answers. Now go through each answer, not only the right answer, and find out why each one is right or wrong. Do this systematic analysis of each question over and over again for each section, for each test, for the study period. You can see how by the end of twelve to sixteen weeks you will be a champ on the MCAT. You will understand how things are worded specifically to get you to think a certain way. You will understand why certain questions are easy and certain questions are hard. The most important part is that you will see a pattern, kind of like in the movie The Matrix, and you will do extremely well on the exam if you follow this procedure.

Once you found out your total score don't get depressed if you did poorly, and don't be excited if you did great. You need to be humbled by this exam. It can kick any smart person's ass.

Now take a day off after you have completed analyzing your test. You deserve a break. Remember we have to do two exams per week for ten weeks. You need to pace yourself. Medical school and the MCAT is like a marathon not a sprint. Continue this process over and over.

Once you get to week three or four look at your list of AAMC topics to cover for the MCAT. These topics are available on the AAMC website. This lists tells you everything that the MCAT tests on. Not all topics will be on every exam, but they can be, and that is all that matters. If there are many topics that are not covered yet, starting this week you will begin to cover two to three additional topics on that list that weren't covered in the exam. How does this look? If a topic says "life cycle of the cell" - then you're going to youtube, google, wikipedia and use resources to learn about the life cycle of the cell such as mitosis and meiosis. The Kahn Academy - a free fantastic resource is available on youtube and at www.kahnacademy.com. There are various lecturers that walk you through a topic in lecture format as they annotate slides.

For the next eight to twelve weeks you will continue to do two exams per week, scoring them, reviewing them, checking off the AAMC list of topics, and doing a few extra topics not yet covered by your exams. Then at week ten you will take a break. No MCAT for week ten and eleven. Now if you have stuck to the schedule, great! If you haven't then you may not be able to take this break, and the break is important. It will help your brain rest. Athletes do it before a big tournament, they rest up and take it easy. They don't train as hard the last days before an event. This is called tapering. If you are someone who planned a twelve to sixteen week cycle like I suggested and stuck to it, then you will go on doing exams at two per week - and even use earlier exams form week one to re-review. Now LISTEN CAREFULLY. The last week before the exam - whether you did the ten, twelve, or sixteen week cycle, you will need to rest the last 3 days before the exam. No more than one to two hours of review per day, but no more. You're brain needs rest and trust me you will need it with all the adrenaline pumping through your vessels on exam day. It is a long day and you need to save up every bit of energy you can. Spend these last 3 days driving to the exam site making sure you know where you will be parking. Pack some lunches, snacks, and drinks for exam day. Make sure it's not some ethnic food you haven't had before, and don't plan to have foods or drinks that you have never tried before. You want to keep everything the same as much as you can. This is an important test and take it seriously. You don't want to get the runs on exam day, or get sick because you didn't listen to my advice. You don't want to get jacked on caffeine and then crash half way through the exam and be so jittery you can't type your responses. I had a student in my medical school class like that. What a wreck. The guy was running into walls the last few days before exams because he was so jacked on caffeine. Not a pretty sight. Yes, and people like this get into medical school. Another thing you want to do before exam day is make sure you sleep at least eight hours. Try to watch a funny movie or do something that you love. Research shows that memory and recall is much easier if you are relaxed compared to if you are stressed. When you go to exam day arrive at least 30 minutes before check in time. Just in case you have a flat tire and your taxi doesn't show. Things can go wrong and they usually do on exam day. So show up early. You should have had enough sleep anyways.

DIAMOND - NEVER (try not to) talk to other students on exam day - especially the MCAT.

During exam day, keep to yourself in the hallways, or even a bathroom stall if you need. Don't make eye contact, don't make small talk. You are a lion and you are chasing your prey - this is not the time to stop and discuss your mothers birthday, how much you studied, or how nervous you are. The other idiots will be doing that, sizing each other up, stressing each other out. You never see me on exam day in a hall way talking. I come early, hide out, and then walk in at the end after everyone is almost checked in. After the exam when I'm finished, I walk straight out, go to the gym, shower and spend time with my kids, and then celebrate that night.   Even through medical school and licensing exams - keep it the same. You are a LION. Do you think a lion checks in with other people before attacking it's prey vs hunting for his next meal? When there is a baseball or hockey championship game do you think the teams hang out and talk to one another before they step out on the field or ice?

"You are a lion in a field of lions - will you rise to the occasion to get your prey or will you give in to fear?"

~Anonymous

Don't have time to study for the MCAT? Give up now. Quit. I have no sympathy for people who say they don't have time to study, or just want to take a $1500 review course. Think about this. Your degree takes four years to complete and well over $20,000. You MCAT is so important the least you could do is spend 1/10 the time on it as you did your degree right? Spend the time, get the grades, and get into medical school.

In summary, do a twelve week cycle at minimum to study for the MCAT. Do two exams per week, score, review, and check AAMC list of topics. Don't worry if you didn't get all the topics by exam date. Just make sure you have covered 65% of them at minimum. Then the last week before the exam, REST, go to your exam site, prepare your food, and lastly have faith in your abilities. If you did what I told you and you believe in yourself - you will do great. Have courage and faith. You need to be strong and tough for an exam like this. It demands it, rise to the occasion. Congratulations you are getting closer to your dream and goals.

Chapter 12 - Money Matters

So now that you and your parents are getting a picture into what it will take for you to get into medical school, I hope you are inspired that there is a plan, and that you can do it if you are willing to put the work into it. Now a major part of applying and planning for medical school involves money.

<u>Pre-Med - the Billion dollar industry.</u>

Like I said in my introduction, and in the last chapter, I'm not a big fan of Kaplan, Princeton and all the other MCAT review series out there. They are just trying to make money off students. In addition to these companies, so many of the big universities have guidance counsellors that don't have a clue on how to plan for university programs like medicine, nursing or dentistry. I tried them multiple times and didn't get anywhere. Then there are the high school guidance counsellors, again so many of them have no clue on how to get into medical school or professional programs. They have a lot of general advice about a lot of programs, but no great advice for students who need a focused laser like plan. Don't forget this profession is something you will be doing the rest of your life - do you want to take that risk by not having a plan? Ask anyone who is successful and see if they didn't have a plan? Underneath all greatness is a plan and hard work.

There are so many people that want to steal your money. The big universities suck you in with their big gyms, prestigious awards, and marketing, but at the end of the day if your kids gets a degree from Harvard and is working at a convenience store, is that the goal? If that happens you'll feel that was a huge waste of $50,000 to $100,000. They don't want you to know what I have already taught you and what I will continue to teach you. They want you to spend more money doing more degrees... they are businesses after all. Universities are not government run institutions that are free, so why not demand more?

If you read this book and do what I tell you - you should be able to save at least $20,000 of the money I wasted. By going to a small university, not doing multiple degrees, only applying to a few schools that you have a chance of getting into, and not wasting money on prep courses. You should also be saving many years compared to me now that you have a plan.

Don't be a Cheap Ass

Now on the flip side of things, I don't want you to be cheap. If there is something I suggest, such as text books, laptops, apps, sports programs, and other opportunities, SPEND THE MONEY. I want you to spend money wisely, don't waste it. You will most likely need to invest $25,000 - $50,000 to get into medical school but it will be worth it once you're in. I don't sit up at night and think about the $60,000 I spent getting in and the $142,000 spent during medical school. Not one second. I write this book with a clean conscious and am telling you, money is just another tool in your toolbox, just like me and this book. Sometimes you pick out a screw driver and say "screw it", other times you pick up a hammer and "kill it", and sometimes you will need to pick up the credit card and say "lets' do it".

Average cost for your undergraduate degree

Item	Cost for 4 years
University/ College Tuition - Undergraduate	$17,000
Rent	$48,000
Food, clothes/ misc	$28,800
MCAT and Prep	$2,000
Volunteer / Sport activities	$1,000
Medical school applications/ Interviews	$3,000
computer/technology/supplies	$3,000
Total expenditures	$102,800

*Rent - $1000/month, Food $500/month, other $100/month

Average Cost of Medical School in Canada

Item	Cost / yr	Total cost
Tuition*	$15,000	$60,000
Books, medical supplies	$600	$2,400
Food	$7,200	$28,800
Accommodations	$12,000	$48,000
Computer/Phone/technology**	$700	$2,800
Total	$35,500	$142,000

*Average of medical schools in Canada

** Computer/technology one time purchase divided over 4 years

You can see how the fees can add up quickly. This is just a rough picture of the costs. The major costs associated with living expenses and food can be reduced considerably if you are living at home, or with friends. Not having to pay rent or food costs would lower your costs of getting an undergraduate degree by approximately $65,000.

In summary don't waste your money on things that won't help you achieve your goal. But don't be cheap either. If you need it to help achieve your goal - then spend it.

Paying for Medical School

Medical school is expensive as shown in the table above. It used to be $5000/yr in the 1990's and now in 2015 is an average of $15,000 per year for three to four years. Abroad this could cost $30,000 - $80,000/year. Thankfully I hear that students loans and banks will help you pay for your tuition abroad as well.

Student Loans

Most student loans come as either state/provincial loans and national loans. In Canada there are national student loans and provincial students loans that can help with the cost of tuition. Usually it's enough to cover your yearly tuition plus some extra. Again it depends on your need and your income. If you're parents are wealthy and they give you money as corporate deductions from their company - you will not get any funding.

Bank Loans - AKA Credit Lines

All the major banks provide student loans from $200,000 - $300,000 for the 4 years. Some give it to you upfront - some give it to you in $50,000 increments so you don't spend it all in your first year. All you need is your acceptance letter and a document from the university saying you are enrolled in medicine. It's scary how easy it is, but I keep hearing from banks that they "love doctors because they pay their debts". Also doctors have a stable income that is almost recession proof.

Parents, Family and Savings.

This section is self explanatory. Give lots of hugs to your parents and family and see if you have any relatives or grandparents that are willing to loan you some money for medical school. The only benefit of this is not having to pay interest when you are done. When you are finished with medical school the government and bank loans will start taking payments from your bank or credit line.

If you have savings for your previous employment or scholarships, this is a good time to use your funds. Don't forget every dollar you take out of the bank you will have to pay back, so be mindful when spending. On the flip side make sure you have a good time too and enjoy medical school. If that means using some of your money to help you take care of yourself with gym memberships, trips, conferences, or that bike you always wanted, go for it. It's all about balance. Only you will know deep inside what that means.

Total expenditures - why you should take your decision seriously

If we combined all the fees from an undergraduate degree and a medical degree, we would have a total expenditure of over $240,000. I want you to re-read that number. It maybe way more if you are a big spender and like new clothes, Starbucks daily, have expensive gym memberships, a nice car, and need to hit the spa a few times a month.

I want you to see that this is a HUGE investment in yourself. After all this money has been spent you still will not have earned any income until residency begins. This is another reason to make sure you plan your career well from high school. Every year you waste or are not focused is another year where you spend more money and make less money.

Residency Income - Money in, less out!

During residency you no longer pay large tuition fees, and the best part is you get an income. This depends on which province you are in. On average a medical resident can make between $45,000 - $57,000/ year. This will feel like a huge relief because your student loans, credit lines, and personal savings will have taken a large hit by now.

Physician Income - Are you sure doctors can make that much?

So after 10 years of undergraduate school, medical school, and residency to be a family doctor you can start to earn between $150,000 - $650,000/ year. The typical family doctor earns about $1000-$2500/day. This depends on how many hours a week you work, how many patients you see per day, whether you work in an urban or rural area, and what province you live in. In 2015 Alberta has one of the highest renumeration for a medical visit compared to other Canadian provinces.

Specialists can have a wide range of incomes as well. Plastic Surgery, Dermatology, Gastroenterology, and Ophthalmology are among the highest paid because of the procedures they do. Some ophthalmologists are bringing in over $2,500,000 per year or more. That's a great income and for some of you this will be a major reason that you will be willing to spend 13-17 years of your life in post secondary education.

As you can see, your $240,000 of debt can be paid off quickly when you're finished, depending on how hard you want to work. This is why many doctors will tell a medical student or resident who is worried about their debt - "don't worry you'll pay it off in the first few years".

Chapter 13 - The Application

After you have completed your high school, are in your third year of undergraduate training, have a great GPA, and have taken the MCAT, it's now time to apply. If you don't have the above pre-requisites stop and try to see how you can attain those items.

If you're not a little nervous after all the information you have received, you're crazy. You should be nervous, it doesn't have to disable you, but being nervous means that what you're fighting for is important. You being a warrior isn't easy and now you are coming up to a major battle and things could go either way. Use your nervous energy to get you pumped up, to train harder, to practise and learn more. Sharpen that axe that we talked about earlier in the book.

Remember the application is step 1 of the Medical school admission process. Step 2 is the Interview. Your application will be very similar no matter what medical school you apply to. It will take a long time to complete the forms and provide the necessary documentation. For this reason I recommend students start early or even the day the application process opens, so that they don' have to rush to get everything together prior to the application deadline. Also taking your time helps you build a solid application. Start looking at the medical school websites for admissions criteria and when the applications open. Get familiar with the schools and what they require. Don't forget to read the fine print. Most applications will require a ton of demographic data, work history, education history, volunteer history, publications/research, honours and awards, references, and an essay. Every school differs but if you can read this book you can read the information on the application process.

Start with one school and do the following steps

1. Go to the admissions website and start an online application

2. Pay the application fee

3. To get yourself rolling - fill out the demographic information - your address, your phone number etc.

4. Start organizing your reference letters (see below)

Reference Letters

So many people ask me about reference letters for medical school and what makes a good letter. I have advice that is sometimes difficult to take for most students and their families.

The best letter is not the one that says:

"Ziang was a wonderful researcher in my lab and she was the best student I have had ever. She was awesome. I think she would be a great doctor."

To me this isn't specific, it doesn't show improvement, skills that we are looking for in the profession.

A good letter is something that highlights the abilities of a student and even dares to talk about weaknesses. An example of a strong letter would have something like the following.

"Raman worked in my medical office for the past 4 months as a medical office assistant. During that time she was able to display her critical thinking abilities in difficult scenarios such as with patients who were demanding and rude. She showed her strengths as an individual and stood her ground. This strength of character as a young woman would be a valuable asset to her future medical practise. Difficult patients are something I see on a regular basis in my clinic. Raman is also personable and recognizes her weaknesses. One of these is her level of compassion. She is very kind and caring to individuals of all walks of life including the vulnerable populations that I see in my clinic. Sometimes she spends time after hours finding shelters for some of these patients. Although this is an asset it may also be a weakness as she will need to learn ways be able to make time for herself and her family in the future."

As you can see in the last letter the writer talks about strengths and weaknesses and the weakness is actually another strength that many of us struggle with. The letter also sheds light on Raman as an individual and talks about her character and her dedication to humanity.
A good reference letter doesn't have to be from a medical doctor, it can be from a neighbour, a coach, or a teacher. Some schools now specifically request that some letters come from individuals other than a medical doctor. Reference letters with breadth from various parts of your life are the best. Think about the interviewers like me that sit for hours reading applications. The best letters are the UNIQUE ones and the ones that tell a STORY. Make sure your reference letter comes from

someone who can tell a story about you that will make everyone smile.

Lastly, don't think that all people you ask for a letter will write you a good letter. I have met a few people who have actually written hurtful demeaning letters for students. I personally don't think this is fair. I would rather take the honest approach and let students know that I would not be able to write them a *strong* letter. These letters can be a deal breaker for many students. Make sure you know the person you are asking to write you a letter. Make sure they don't write something like:

"I only met this person for a four day rotation through my clinic and feel that I can't provide an informative letter for him. He seems nice, but I'm unable to truly evaluate his abilities. I wish him all the best in his career".

This type of letter coming from the dean of a medical school is not a good letter. The student might feel thankful that he has the dean of a medical school writing her a reference letter, but if the content sucks, you are worse off than asking your neighbour to write you a letter of support.

DIAMOND -Reference letters are another way the interview committee gets to know you. It is a crucial step in your application. CHOOSE WISELY.

Essay

Most schools ask you to write an essay about why you want to be a doctor, or describing a time in your life that you faced adversity. The essay is more the "artsy" component of your application. This is where you get to shine. You get to talk about yourself and sell yourself. Yes I said sell. If you can't sell yourself, your letter is going to suck. This is the time you need to not only tell the committee all the things you have done, but talk about you as a person. Tell them YOUR STORY. The story needs to be unique. Every application talks about volunteering in hospitals or with lower socioeconomic status individuals. So many applications talk about how they "want to help people". Imagine reading that over and over again, and the next person talks about something totally different. Something like the following.

"I lost my Mom when I was 13, she was my best friend. I would give anything to see her again. I wish she would see me apply to medical school and achieve my dreams. She was a dreamer and now I see so much of her in me. As much as I would like to tell you about all the things I've done, I'd rather tell you about my life. Let me take you on a journey of why I want to practice medicine."

This is an introduction that would grab my attention. This is unique. I want to know more, I want to read more. That is your goal.

DIAMOND - your essay should tell your story and your story should be unique.

Just to give you an idea of what an essay can look like I have added my essay from my application to residency below. It is something that I consider to be unique. When I got to my interviews, every interviewer thanked me for my letter and said how "refreshing it was" to read my letter. That's your goal

Dr. Kaler's admission letter to family medicine residency

I have wanted to practice Family Medicine from the first day of medical school. I knew that communities need Family Physicians who can quarterback health care, but also act as advocates and leaders for change. Having the trust of patients and a community is a special gift that physicians have been entrusted with, but sometimes take for granted. It is our role to take care of communities, to encourage and develop healthier citizens, and most importantly, to start by taking care of ourselves and leading by example.

Growing up in Alberta as an only child I was thankful I had loving parents, and good friends. I was always encouraged to play competitive sports such as tennis, downhill ski racing, hockey, and basketball. Now, as a parent, I realize that it was an excellent way to keep me busy and out of trouble, but more importantly, provided me with leadership and decision-making skills. Until the age of 26 I had everything any young person could ask for, yet I still lacked the internal drive needed to intensely pursue a specific goal. Basically, I wasn't able to "give it everything". Then one minute, one day, my world changed forever. My father, my best friend, my angel - passed away.

I struggled for a year trying to find my way, trying to feel grounded and some sense of place in a world that seemed so cold. Clinically, I was depressed. Emotionally, I was broken. My friends slipped away and were busy and involved in their daily activities, and I felt alone...

After spending the majority of 2006 in this state I found my drive, my passion, my determination return but in a deeper more meaningful way. I recognized that my experience of darkness had brought me closer to myself. I decided that maybe I could support others, maybe I could be an advocate for change, and maybe - just maybe - I could dream again. It was then that I saw what I never saw before: the practice of medicine - it had been there waiting for me. I had friends in medicine, my mother volunteered in medicine for 20 years, and my father received 10 years of life from medicine, but also died at the hands of medical error. My wife was in medicine and starting residency - could it be more obvious? I stopped and critically appraised my decision - thinking about the pros and cons: "could I do this? I've tried so many times before and it's so hard to get in? I'm 30? I'll be 36 when I'm done? I have kids - will I see them?" Then I had a conversation with my wife. She asked me one simple thing - would I rather be doing something that I don't like and wondering what could have been, or try to get into medical school and know that I was giving myself a turn. I knew what I needed to do. So many of us, including me, spend so much of our lives encouraging others, supporting others, and giving everything to others - our friends, our families, our children - and in that entire journey we forget to give back to ourselves. This may sound selfish, but it is deeper than that. It is actually as unselfish as we can get. With insight into this statement, one will realize that it is through self-care and introspection that we are truly able to care for another. I recognized this, and decided to take a chance on me.

I did my pre-requisites, wrote the MCAT, applied and started medical school in 2010 at Dalhousie University. Over the course of the past 4 years I have come to realize that medicine is a gift. It provides us with many opportunities to give to others on various levels, but it also gives us the chance to see how much we are alike. How many of us want similar things in life - love, happiness, relationships, stability, and the need to belong. Many of the patients I worked with reminded me of the lesson I learned when my father passed: that we all come across darkness, but we are able to find the light if we truly see what is inside us and the unawakened potential that is there. If we see that light, we can be the leaders that we are inspired and aspiring to be. We learn that the simple things in life - a hug, holding someones hand when they pass away, sitting quietly while a new baby is being born, and sleeping and eating well - can provide us with a sense of well-being that can't be purchased. It is always there just waiting to be seen.

Why do I speak so philosophically during my personal letter to the Calgary Family Medicine program? Because this is who I am: I am a leader, a dreamer, and someone who has recognized that medicine is a part of me, just like my extremities, just like my passion for sport and the outdoors. Instead of listing details of my achievements and accomplishments, I thought I would highlight to you what I am most proud of - my journey.

I dream of being a family physician who is a leader in my community throughout the continuum of life, to be a father *who my daughters see make mistakes but learn from them, and being a guide on the mountainous path of life.*

Respectfully,

Dr. Norry Kaler BSc MSc MD

I don't want you to think this is how you should write your letter. I want you to get an idea of how a letter can be unique. It can take someone on a journey. It can let them peek into your life. The essay is a key part to your application. It is your moment to tell the committee who you are. Go for it! Be brave and be unique.

Chapter 14 - The interview process

Be humble, be yourself and your only job is...

My most important recommendation is to be yourself and don't BORE the interviewer. Make sure they are fighting themselves to stop smiling when you leave the room. The only way they will do that is if you are smiling and excited. Be passionate about yourself and selling yourself. If you're not - then how are they going to score you. They basically have to decide if they like you or not. You're job is to make them like you A LOT! Be excited and enthusiastic. Isn't that someone you want to talk to? Or do you want the dry boring person to hang out with you tonight?

I'm still surprised at some of the dry people in my medical school class or residency class. They can't communicate, are too scared to stand up for anything, and they're quiet. So BORING.

Here are some tips to be excited and passionate.

1. Visualize yourself getting in to medical school before the interview. Imagine you are doing great in the interview and they want to just tell you in the interview how great you are - but they can't. Imagine the interviewing wanting to spend time with you later to hear more about your story.

2. Be confident and believe in your abilities. Talk to yourself in the months leading up to the interview. Tell yourself how great you are, and how proud you are of your accomplish-ments. You need to learn how to portray yourself with confi-

dence and that means learning how to be humble AND proud of what you have done. Being a doctor requires many skills - one of which is to advocate for your patients. How are you going to advocate for them if you can't advocate for yourself?

3. Be a good listener. When the interviewer is talking or another simulated patient is talking, just be quiet and listen. Take notes (on paper and pencil provided) - and then respond after a silence.

4. Don't be afraid of awkward silences. Use these to your advantage. Most people are running in to the interview rooms and rushing through the interview. Your job is to at 1 or 2 points in the interview to take 5 seconds to reflect and say. "I'm going to take a few seconds to review".   Then be silent - reflect - even if internally you're freaking out. Then start up again. This shows a level of wisdom that many applicants don't have. Showing the ability to be calm in a stressful situation is something doctors do on a daily basis.

5. Dress Nice - look the best you can look. Suit and tie is a must for males, and typically a business casual attire for women. Nothing too provocative as some interviewers can be put off by this and take marks off for un-professionalism.

6. Many times there is NO RIGHT ANSWER. So many of the medical students I have seen and interviewed are always looking for the right answer. The interviewer isn't looking for that - but rather your ability to formulate and articulate a viewpoint, and to see both sides of a topic. Be respectful, but don't be afraid to pick one side of an argument and roll with it - just maintain professionalism at all times.

7. Make eye contact - so many people who lack confidence just won't make eye contact. They will look around a room. 65-75% of our language is non-verbal, if you're not looking at the interviewer they can't pick up on your cues and may start to feel like you lack confidence, we don't want that.

8. Practise. Find a friend, parent, or family member who will be willing to give you critical feedback. Be able to tell you that you were good at something, but more importantly where you need to improve. You need to get rocked once in a while and then use that experience to improve. Practise with these people who can be critical of you. I train students all the time and I'm hard on them. I want them to walk into a real interview feeling they have been able to deal with my feedback, so that they feel more confident on interview day.

9. BREATHE. I know sounds lame, but it has been proven to calm you down. Take a breath when you read each station scenario, then breath again before you get into a room. When you hear the buzzer to go into the room of an MMI format interview, walk in slow. Be composed. Relax- or at least pretend. This first few second will set the tone of the interview.

10. Let go. Don't try too hard. It's obvious to interviewers if you are. The best interviews are those that you feel relaxed and feel like you're just talking to an old friend. The only way to do this is to let go of your ego. Try to think of yourself as someone who is just going through the motions and that whatever will be will be. You've done your part. You've trained for this day for a long time and now it's here. Let go of the pressure and stress.

Chapter 15 - Getting rejection letters

Okay, this is where many of you will end up if you don't do fantastic on you MCAT, and your undergraduate degree. You will then have to make a decision on what to do now that you got a rejection letter. Here are some of your options and my honest opinion.

Many of you may have done extremely well on your MCAT and undergraduate courses and still not receive an admission. Many students have applied 2-3 times to get into medical school in North America. Be patient and keep trying if you have done the things I have outlined in this book and you are competitive.

"It's been a hard days work"

That song by the Beatles encapsulates it all. If you show you have been working hard it will only be an asset to your application. Hopefully you have taken my suggestion and have a Nursing, Education, Pharmacy, Physiotherapy, Nutrition, or other professional degree that can get you a wonderful job. If you don't get in and you have one of these degrees under your belt here are your options.

1. Go and work. Stop schooling for a year - go and make some money. See what it feels like to have a full time, well paying job. Pay off some of your debt and spend some money on things you wanted to do like travelling, buying a nice bike, or car if you can afford it!

2. Upgrading - If you're grades were not 85%, 3.7/4.0 or better then you may consider going back to school and upgrading. This is where you go to a smaller school again like I suggested earlier - and you take 10 courses between September and May that are upper level (3rd/4th year). Remember summer courses don't count to part of your GPA to many medical schools. Find classes with less than 30 people in them. Take courses that you like, but are also easy to do well in. Nutrition, arts courses, music courses, and education. How do you know you will do well. Go 1 month before the semester begins and find out who will be teaching the courses. Talk to them and get to know them. Ask them about the course. If they seem like a nice individual ask them flat out - "if I work hard in this course can I do well". Show interest. This is what I did. I actually registered in 14 courses (7 per semester)- tried them for the first 2 weeks and then dropped the courses I didn't like. Smaller schools are open to this, larger ones may not be - look into this.

3. Volunteer - I'm not a huge fan of this option. It's a good idea if you want to add some volunteering on the side, but to take a year off and volunteer can be a good/ bad thing. Here's why. It shows you don't need to work. You have access to money, and you didn't really go out on your own and become an independent person. It may look very good on your application to show that you worked with doctors without borders, or Unicef, but if I'm interviewing I want to find people who have maturity. This means being unique, which is working, volunteering, paying debt, and having to make difficult decisions. Again this is a tricky one. I'll let you play this out the way you want to.

4. Graduate Degree

A graduate degree is a Masters MSc, MA, or a Doctor of Philosophy - PhD. In my opinion. Don't do it. If you read other medical school admissions books they will actually tell you to consider this. This is why I can't stand people who don't have a clue about the admissions process giving advice to you.

How do I know? Because I have a Masters degree remember? I got one point out of a possible one hundred points for doing a 2.5 year degree. This was at three schools I applied to. If you would have told me that before I did the degree, do you think I would have gone through all that work? NO! I would have done upgrading, a degree that could get me a job, or gone on vacation. I had 4 publications and still it provided me with a negligible increase in my pre-interview score.

DO NOT DO A GRADUATE DEGREE. Unless you want to be a researcher, this is not a smart idea. Once you are in medicine and you want to do research - go for it. But remember you're not in medicine - that's why you're reading this book. If you are already doing a graduate degree then you most likely should finish, or find a unique way out that doesn't look bad on your application. Once you start a graduate degree, it will most likely reflect poorly on you if you quit.

How long do I keep trying

If you are desperate like I was - you never stop. You just go as hard as you can. Most important thing is that you have a plan. You know what you're doing and you have followed all the suggestions in my book. If something isn't working it is important to figure out what isn't working so that you can continue to improve your application. Don't make the mistake I did of listening to others who are in medical school or doctors in your community. Many don't have any idea of what they are doing or talking about.

You need to continue to change and enhance your application every year. If you apply with the same application you got rejected with and don't change it what do you think will happen the following year?

Chapter 16 - Deciding to go Abroad for Medicine

This chapter was written with the generous contributions of Dr. Iain Law BSc, MA, MD, and 2 other anonymous contributors. All of these individuals went abroad to complete their medical school training and then obtained a residency position in Canada.

This chapter is one of the longest chapters in my book. The main reason is that it is one of the most requested topics for me to discuss from students and parents. Sadly very few people see the flaws with going abroad for medicine.

The Canadian Residency Matching Service (CaRMS) report that there are approximately 3500 Canadian students studying abroad. This is a large number of students considering there are approximately 2700 students studying medicine in Canada! These 3500 students attended 55 different schools outside of North America. The number of students has increased exponentially since 2000. 90% of these applicants report going abroad so that they can return to practise in Canada. The majority of these individuals have $100,000 - $300,000 more debt than the Canadian medical student studying abroad (CSA).

21% of these CSA students have one or more parents that are doctors compared to 16% of Canadian medical students, of these the majority studied in Ireland. Of all the CSA's that applied for residency spots in Canada most come from Ontario, British Columbia, and Alberta. For a more detailed summary of statistics of CSA/IMG's go to www.carms.ca to find more information.

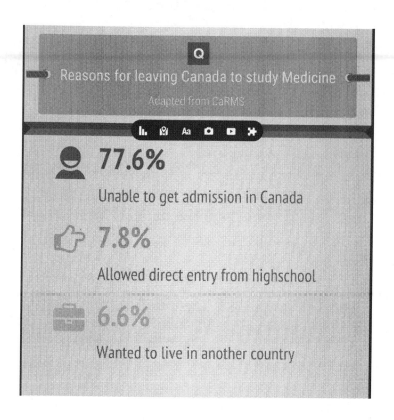

77.6%

Unable to get admission in Canada

7.8%

Allowed direct entry from highschool

6.6%

Wanted to live in another country

So how many times did you apply before you left abroad? The average CSA student applied only 1.7 times before making the decision to go abroad vs. the medical student in Canada having to apply an average of 2.6x before getting in to a Canadian medical school!

Going to medical school abroad has become a billion dollar industry for universities around the world. University of Queensland actively sends recruiters to conferences and events in Canada and the USA to recruit students because of the amount of money students bring into the country. This is occurring around the world and parents and students are willing todo whatever it takes to get that medical degree. However, as you will see in this chapter, one must be weary of this process and be informed before jumping into it. Families can spend up to $500,000 and not be able to return to Canada to practise medicine. It is a risky endeavour that is only becoming riskier. When you have completed your degree and want to return to Canada it will be difficult unless you do very well on your re-qualification exams.

Eventually my recommendation, and from the input from a few doctors that studied abroad and returned, is to try to get in to medical school in North America. Work harder and keep trying to get in in North America using the plan I have provided.

International Medical Graduates - IMG - (Canadian citizens who go abroad to get medical education are still considered international medical graduates) are also known as CSA - Canadians Studying Abroad. Many would support me in saying if they knew how to get into medical school in Canada or had some guidance they would rather stayed in Canada, rather than travel abroad. So many students have travelled abroad, received their MD, only to not be able to practise when they return. The main reason is because they are unable to receive a residency position. Personally, I imagine it is harder to know you have spent $350,000-$500,000 on medical school with little to no chance of being able to practise when you return. Things are only getting harder now with more and more graduates going abroad and having difficulties returning.

<u>"But my education was way better than Canada"</u>

Numerous IMG's have discussions with me stating "we have better training abroad than in Canada", "I know more than the Canadian applicant". This all maybe true however the reality is you need to get through the Canadian system to practise. That's the end of it. Until things change for admissions/ re-entry requirements you are going to need to accept this reality.

DIAMOND - Accept the reality - you will need to get through the Canadian system to practise in Canada if you are an IMG/ CSA. IT WILL BE VERY HARD TO RETURN if you go abroad and it is only getting worse.

Studying for your Canadian Licensing exams while you're abroad and in medical school will be HARD. You will have responsibilities to complete at your medical school, while trying to get the best grades possible on your exams here. Don't forget you will have to come to Canada for some of your exams and take time off from your medical school to do so. Why not put in all that effort in Canada and then not have to worry for the remainder of your career about returning, with this huge weight on your shoulders about getting back into Canada to follow your dreams. You have bascially limited yourself by going abroad and many students didn't even know it.

The difficult part of the medical school process in Canada is "Getting In". The rest is simple. Anyone who tells you otherwise is full of it. If you can get in, you can get through. The medical schools in Canada are so well organized to help you to, not only get through, but excel on the final licensing exam. There are teams of people who have sit down at every medical school and plan out exactly what to teach medical students to make sure they pass the licensing exam in Canada. Why you may ask? Because medical schools are a fantastic collaboration of people who want to win. It's the most competitive group of people I've ever met all sitting and working under one roof. Therefore the collective energy of a medical school is one where the entire school wants to win. A medical school class that does poorly on a national licensing exam reflects poorly on them, and they will do anything to prevent their school name from being tarnished.

In medical school, if you're hardworking (you won't get in if you're not), and do what you are told to do, study for your exams, and act professionally, the school will take care of you.

The flip side is going abroad. Theses schools are easier to get into, but you will have a heavier stress level at the end of your training to return. There is also not as much room for error. When returning to Canada you will need to excel on your licensing exams and if you pass, but don't do great on some of the exams, you are unable to re-write them. YES THATS RIGHT! Read that again. If you pass the exam, but don't do as well as you like, you CANNOT re-write the exam. That means - game over. However, prior to medical school, you can re-write the MCAT, upgrade courses, continue to better yourself to help you get in. I would choose the latter option any-day.

DIAMOND - Get in abroad with a lower threshold criteria and have a little chance of getting back into Canada to practise medicine, or work hard earlier in Canada and the rest is smooth sailing.

The most popular countries (and heavily advertised) for obtaining a medical degree outside of Canada are: Australia, the Caribbean islands, Ireland, Eastern Europe and Asia (India / China).

Let us start by ruling out countries that are not worthwhile going to for the study of medicine in hopes to return to North America.

Eastern Europe and Asia - Poland, Hungary, China, and India.

Poland and Hungary are probably your least advised prospects. This is because they may have english programs in medicine (some do not) but the culture and the community are considerably different than Canada. Why does this matter you ask? Well when you return to do your interviews, and write your exams, the subtle differences in culture will play a role. This maybe in answering a question about Aboriginal health, or ethical dilemmas relevant to Canadian issues, which are on a Canadian board exam, and the OSCE (structured medical interview). These questions may be difficult to answer for the student studying in a considerably different environment.

This is also true for students studying in India and China. Yes you will get the education, you will get clinical experience, but remember that this aspect is only a portion of getting back into Canada to practise medicine. The culture shift is not as dramatic in the UK or Australia since their systems - albeit different - have many similarities to our country. This may create a barrier for your learning and your education. Again we do not want to create hurdles for you to practice medicine in Canada, but opportunities. We want to plan to use the most successful tools available to return.

Remember if you are serious about medicine, travelling abroad is not a travel vacation like I hear from so many students interested in this field. It's not where you go and study for a bit, come back, and become doctor. You are going to have to do well in medical school abroad, get a residency in the US or Canada, which will require you to be extremely well rounded. You will most likely need to have some research, study for licensing exams in Canada and do well on them, all while you're away from home and spending tons of money.

Other reasons to not go to these schools is for safety reasons. Eastern Europe, Asia, and India are fantastic places to travel, but they have slightly higher crime rates and other national agendas that could affect you while you're studying abroad. I'm not willing to take that risk with my kids or myself. My well being is far more important and it should be to you as well.

I think we should easily rule out the Eastern European medical schools based on limited ability to return, safety, variable national stability, and limited viability to work in the country of study. The chances of you being able to work in Poland, Hungary, and even India are limited as there are students from those countries studying medicine that are struggling to find work in their home nations. These countries may not allow you to practise there without being a citizen of the country. If you're interested in staying and working in these countries - please contact those schools and the consulate in those countries to obtain accurate information.

Ireland/ UK

Ireland and the United Kingdom's medical schools also provide some barriers to returning. The tuition fees are extremely high and as are the living expenses. The yearly tuition fees in Ireland are $50,000 - $75,0000 per year, multiply that by 4 and you get approximately $200,000 to $300,000 for a 4 year program. Remember these fees are helping fund these large universities and are providing them with large profit margins. The difficulties accumulate when you realize you CANNOT practise in Ireland once you get your MD. You can't get a residency position (unless you somehow become a citizen). You're only option is to go to medical school and try to get a residency position back in Canada or the US otherwise you won't be practising medicine. That's a lot of time and money money spent to not be successful in your goals.

As the big kahuna's on the popular Canadian and American TV shows, the Dragons Den and Shark Tank would say, "For this reason I'm out".

The Caribbean

From the CaRMS survey of IMG/CSA's the Caribbean schools have the highest numbers of Canadians studying abroad (41.8% of all students). These schools are still like the ones above. You are not guaranteed an internship and the ability to practise medicine. You are paying between $20,000 to $50,000 per year to get a medical degree. Some of the Caribbean schools have affiliations with some US schools to provide them with clerkship years (years 3 and 4 of medical school) in the US which is a unique program that may provide some students with a better chance of getting into the US after completing their medical school training. This is because it will be easier to obtain reference letters from people you have worked with in the US. You will have a better understanding of the US system, which is quite similar to the Canadian system (academically). Students are still required to write both the USMLE 1 and 2. If they pass both of these with excellent marks and apply to the US residency matching service they will increase their chance of obtaining a residency position, but don't forget they don't compete with all American students on a level playing field.

Here are some of the major medical school players in the Caribbean.

• Saba University
• Ross University
• St. George's.
• American Unviersity of the Caribbean

Australia

Australia has 19 medical schools and all of them accept North American students. Some range from $40,000/year to $70,000 per year. Australia trains a lot of doctors, about 1.5 doctors for every 1 in Canada and the US. Many of these are foreign students. Australian citizen students pay considerably lower tuition, averaging about $4000 per year. The MD in Australia is 4 years after obtaining an undergraduate degree, and the MBBS is 6 a year program out of high school. Many students prefer to have the MD, because of the optics associated with these two letters around the world. Students in both streams then must do their residency training on top of this which ranges from 4 to 8 years in Australia depending on the specialty. Family medicine is approximately 4 years to complete. See the Table below for the number of years this route will take to practise in Canada.

The major caveat is that in Australia, up until recently, almost all Canadian and foreign students who
attended Australian medical schools were given a residency position in Australia. They were all provided with a position where they could work, make money, and eventually become a general practitioner (family doctor) or specialist.

So how popular is studying abroad in Australia? In some schools there can be as many as 70 Canadian students in a single medical school class! That is a heck of a lot of Canadians who have gone to Australia and spent over $200,000 to 400,000 dollars for an MD.

Getting a residency spot in Australia was no issue until recent years. Now it appears that capacity has been reached. Now there are fewer residency spots available. When the country needed to decide to choose if an Australian student or foreign students studying medicine in Australia will get a residency spot, undoubtedly the Australian residents will win, and as they should. Therefore perhaps 5 to10 years ago this stream was an excellent choice, but today it maybe a process that you should be anxious about.

Number of years after high school to practising medicine

Schooling	Austriallia	Canada
Undergraduate degree years	4	4
MD years	4	4
Residency matching and Canadian exams	1-2 (avg)	0
Residency Training (Family Med)	4	2
Total years	14	10

The table above explains how many years it would take to complete your training if you went abroad for medicine. If one was to get accepted to Australia after an undergraduate degree and took the quickest route to practising medicine, Canada is 4 years shorter and an average of $200,000 less. In all likelihood students go to Australia after applying in Canada for 2-3 years, or after completing a graduate degree. So in actual fact the typical student will spend even longer compared to their peers in Canada. Of course there are numerous scenarios that are possible. I only want to bring to your attention that if we plan to succeed in Canada from high school onwards, we can save years, money, and stress for a student wanting to go to medicine in Canada.

DIAMOND - Trying to get into medical school in North America will save you time, years, and money - if you're hard working and have a plan. Or you can play roulette and go abroad.

Australia is a great place for people to practice medicine as it is similar to Canada in many regards and residents are paid better than in Canada. Depending on the number of years you have been a resident your salary can range from $70,000 to $150,000 per year. However, as I mentioned above, in recent years Canadian students have been left "unmatched" to a residency spot and have not been able to work. This is only increasing as capacity has been met in rural and urban areas of Australia. This means that soon, Australia too will only open its doors for educating medical students from Canada, but not provide them with residency spots and the opportunity to be employed like Ireland has done.

A doctor who went abroad to Australia explained their story to me which I thought would be very relevant for people thinking about going abroad.

This student knew in his last year of university that she didn't want to apply to medical school in Canada because it was going to be difficult to obtain admission and he didn't want to waste time trying to get in here. When there was a probability he could start studying medicine in Australia in a few months, he applied to medical school in Australia. His intentions were to settling down in Australia after he completed his training.

Australia/Universities pay third party companies to travel and recruit foreign students to study in Australia. One such company, Oztrekk, travels across Canada presenting on studying abroad in Australia. One of the programs they present on is medicine. This student saw this booth at a career fair and decided he was going to apply.

Through this organization, he learned more of the schools in Australia. He provided this company with his application and documentation and they sent the application to his school of choice, which happened to be University of Queensland in Brisbane. Once accepted he packed his bags and moved to Brisbane. In his 1st year he realized how different the systems in Canada were compared to Australia. In Canada we have a 4 year MD program which is comparable to Australia, which has a 4 year MBBS or MD program after you complete an undergraduate degree.

After medical school all medical graduates do a 1 to 2 year mandatory internship/residency. Following this internship you apply to be admitted to the family medicine program if you want to be a family doctor which is another 2 to 4 years of training. In Canada the average medical student takes 6 years to complete medical school and family medicine residency training. For this reason this student decided to try to come back to Canada to be a family physician.

Requirements to study in Australia.

Most schools require a minimum MCAT score and a GPA cut-off to apply to Australian schools. These scores are considerably lower than the average it takes to obtain admission to a Canadian medical school. This student was accepted along with 70 other Canadian students in his class, to Queensland, extrapolating that there was approximately 350 Canadian students in the 4 year program.

Finances and other stuff

As mentioned previously medical schools are expensive abroad. In Australia, tuition prices ranged from $45,000 to $60,000 Canadian per year with almost yearly tuition increases. A four year program would cost approximately $240,000.

The living expenses are also considerable higher with an average meal costing twice as much at a similar restaurant in Canada. Rent is similar to those in the major urban centres in Canada.

CLERKSHIP ROTATIONS DONE IN CANADA BY CSA

★★★★★

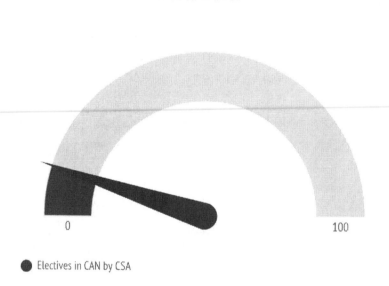

0   100

● Electives in CAN by CSA

IMG/ CSA - returning to Canada - what do I need to do?

When you are in your 2nd year of medical school abroad you will start hoping that you will get electives back in Canada or the US. These electives are what will help drive your application. If you get some electives in Canada, you can then work hard and try to get a reference letter. Why do you need a reference letter from a Canadian Physician? Well think of how it would look if you are applying to CaRMS, a residency matching service for CANADA, with NO references from Canada? It's going to be a lot harder to get in. That's not the only problem though. Getting a clerkship elective in Canada is equally as tough because Canadian programs are struggling to give Canadian medical graduates electives. The IMG/CSA student gets the last pick. Some schools like the University of Calgary won't even consider giving IMG/CSA's an elective. All the individuals who were successful with their applications that helped with this chapter had done 2 elective rotations in Canada.

After completion of your degree or in the last year of medicine you will write some of the Canadian medical exams (I discuss below) and apply to the Canadian Residency Matching Service (CaRMS) as an IMG. To apply to CARMS and to get an interview your scores need to be high on ALL of your exams. Remember the competition is fierce and there are more IMG's than ever.

One of my colleagues suggests that your exam scores need to be in the top 10% of all exam writers. If you get good marks in both exams and if you have applied to many schools and received interviews then you know you have a solid application. If you have applied for years and not gotten an interview something needs to be addressed on your application. Sadly your exam scores you will not be able to fix once you pass them and receive a low score.

You're grades need to be top notch to be able to compete with your peer IMG/CSA students who are also desperately trying to get in. If you are going to do this route you should apply to almost all the programs that will accept IMG graduates in Canada. This is a good screening method to see how many places accept your application and give you an interview. If you get numerous interviews then your application must be strong.

I am still surprised how pick some IMG/CSA students are on where they apply to medicine and where they do their residency. "I only want to apply to Alberta". Some of these people I counselled before I went to medical school and they still aren't practising, and are only apply to Alberta programs? If you want something bad enough you have to go all out to get it. Obviously this person doesn't want it bad enough.

Returning to Canada - Hoops to jump through

For the Canadian medical student, the most difficult part of the journey will be trying to get in to medical school. Once you get admission into medical school, you will have to work, but not as hard as getting into MD school. I compare applying to medical school for the Canadian student to applying to CaRMS for the IMG/CSA student. Their difficulty will be trying to get back into Canada to study medicine, which I feel the odds are far worse than applying to medical school in Canada.

Students must write and be successful at the MCCEE and the NAC OSCE exams to be considered for an interview as an IMG to a Canadian medical residency program. Here is some explanation on each exam.

MCCEE - Qualifying exam # 1

A student would prospectively write their MCCEE (Medical Council of Canada Evaluating exam) in the country they reside in (exam can be written abroad at certain test centres). This is a 4 hour long exam that is computer based. It has 180 multiple choice questions. The score is scaled exam with a low score of 50 and a high score of 500. Average scores are 270. Students will need to obtain at least a 350-400 out of 500 on this exam to be competitive. If you fail this exam you can re-write it, but if you pass this exam you can not re-write it. This is crucial for you to know before you leave to study abroad. Imagine you go abroad for 4-6 years get your MD, spend $500,000 write your MCCEE exam, pass and get a low score, let's say 275. You WILL NEVER BE ABLE TO RE-WRITE the exam. Which also means you most likely will probably never get a residency spot in Canada. That's a lot riding on one test. Most IMG students write this exam in their 4th year of medical school in their country of study. Your school MUST be listed on the International Medical Education Directory for you to be eligible to write this exam, check the following link here to see if your school is listed. imed.faimer.org.

DIAMOND - IF you pass the MCCEE and don't do well - You cannot re-write the exam. Are you willing to take that risk after being away for 4 years, $500,000 spent, and all the pressure on 1 exam that you can't re-write if you fail?

NAC - OSCE - Qualifying exam # 2

The NAC OSCE (National Assesment Collaboration Objective Structured Clinical Exam) is a series of clinical examination based on medicine, obstetrics, gynecology, psychiatry, and surgery. You need to have passed the MCCEE to write this exam. The scoring is on a scale of 0-100. You need a score of 80 to be competitive. The exam can be taken a maximum of 3 times, and only once per year. Again if you pass this exam you CANNOT re-write it. It is NOT a scaled exam, your score is your score. Students will need to fly back to Canada to write the NAC OSCE in Canada. This is usually during their school year and students will have to take time to fly back to Canada while still preparing for exams in Australia or other countries.

DIAMOND - you need to pass the MCCEE to write the NAC. If you pass, it is your FINAL score. No upgrading or re-writes. Maximum of 3 attempts if you fail.

MCCQE1 - Practising in Canada

Finally after being accepted as a resident to a program the student must write the MCCQE 1 (Medical Council of Canada Qualifying Examination 1) that all Canadian students write at the end of their medical training prior to starting residency. You must be in the last part of your medical training to be eligible to write this exam. You also must have passed the MCCEE. IMG students must also write this exam prior to starting residency once they are accepted to a residency program. Some students I spoke with wrote this exam shortly after writing the MCCEE exam since there was some overlap between the two tests. This prevented them from having to re-learn the information again later in the year.

Costs of Examinations

These tests are expensive MCCEE is $1695, the NAC OSCE is $2230, and the MCCQE1 is $1470. This does not include travel and expenses incurred to write these exams. Alberta applicants need to do 1-2 additional tests.

Applying as an IMG to US States and Provinces - "Residency status"

To apply to certain states and provinces many residency programs require that you to be a "resident" of that province. This means you need to have lived there a certain amount of time and meet their requirements for being a "resident".

For example Alberta is one such province. You cannot apply for an IMG spot to the University of Calgary or University of Alberta unless you are a resident of Alberta. To meet this requirement you need to have the following:

Eligibility requirements for residency positions in Alberta
• Be a Canadian Resident or Citizen
• Have an IMED medical degree.
• Alberta residency for 6 months or 2 years of Alberta High School, or 2 years of Alberta post secondary education.
• English Language proficiency, IELTS, TOEFL, etc.
• Pass the MCCEE

In Nova Scotia Canada you need to meet the eligibility requirements for their province and provide a "return of service" contract to work in the maritimes for 2-5 years. This varies on the province you are signing this agreement with.

Nova Scotia also has a unique program for IMG's to apply to clerkship and re-complete their 3rd and 4th years of medical school at Dalhousie. Once they are completed - they are considered a Dalhousie graduate and enter the first iteration of CaRMS.

There are many unique situations that are available. Please look into the provinces and states you would like to apply to and READ the fine print.

Other Considerations of Travelling and Studying Abroad

Insurance

Health insurance is something you will have to pay to your school to cover you for your basic needs. Any surgeries or hospital admissions would cost you out of pocket and these bills can add up quickly. Car insurance and a vehicle are not 100% necessary. Public transportation system is quite good in the larger centres at most urban centres around the world and is far better than North American public transport.

How do I get money to study abroad?

The banks in Canada will provide up to $250,000 in loans as a credit line. Some of the hiccups include the need for it to be cosigned by a parent or family member. Alberta student loans provides residents of Alberta with up to $35,000 per year to study as well. Other provinces are sticky and will not support students going abroad or will give lesser amounts. Those students coming from provinces other than Alberta will need to arrange enough money to afford the living expenses and tuition fees that their credit line does not cover.

Successful IMG 2007-2015

Successful IMG   unsuccessful IMG

This is a major hurdle for many people who can not afford to spend $300,000 to $500,000 on an medical degree in a foreign country without guarantee of the ability to return to work. In comparison, the cost to go to medical school in Canada is $100-$150,000 for a 4 year degree including expenses. Canadian students have access to $250,000 from banks and $20,000 to 30,000 per year in funds from the federal and provincial student loan programs. This should be adequate to cover the majority of costs and more.

Finally, you have jumped through all the hoops, what are your chances of returning? What are the statistics in Canada today? In the past 5 years an average of only 5% of IMG/CSG applicants get accepted to residency positions. That is out of all the students that qualified to apply! That means passing the MCCEE, NAC OSCE, applying to CaRMS, getting interviews, and then getting matched (accepted).

Conclusion about Studying Abroad for Medical School

In summary don't go abroad. If you have the motivation, ability to work hard, and a plan as I lay out in this book you will have an excellent chance to get into medical school in Canada. Going abroad is expensive, and provides the largest hurdle when trying to return to Canada to obtain a residency position. I would argue that any of the students who went abroad and obtained a position in Canada after returning would have been accepted to medical school with the plan I laid out in my book. To do extremely well on the licensing exams in Canada is not an easy task.

Chapter 17 - Special Populations and Circumstances

There are a few populations that have special considerations when applying to medical schools and I want to make sure you are aware of them.

<u>Aboriginal Applicants</u>

I have a soft place in my heart of Aboriginal students. I have two close friends that are Aboriginal physicians and I know quite a few more. They are all wonderful people who have accomplished so much in their short careers. Many of them are involved in their community, politics, and are serving Aboriginal peoples across the nation.

Many Aboriginal applicants will have a successful admission to medical school if they meet the minimum requirements to apply to medical schools. Almost all medical schools in Canada and some in the US have spots reserved for Aboriginal students that no one else can compete for. The number of applicants that are Aboriginal are sadly still quite low. Usually only 6-10 applications for 3-6 spots at some schools. Aboriginal students still need to meet the minimum criteria at all schools. This means that if one school requires the MCAT, a minimum GPA of 3.5/4.0, and an undergraduate degree, Aboriginal applicants must meet this criteria too.

When admitted to medical school as an Aboriginal student, there are pools of funding that will provide you with some pockets of money to help. If you are Metis - this is far less (if any at all), and you will have to support yourself with a student loan or line of credit from the bank. If you are status first nation from a reserve, you should receive full support from your community. Ask, if they turn you down, keep pushing and demand them to support you. Feel free to email me if you have other questions about this pool of applicants or if you would like to get in touch with an Aboriginal physician to speak to your personally.

Minority Applicants

Individuals who are of African descent and/or Hispanic have reserved seats in some of the state colleges and universities in the US. Many schools in Canada have an mandate to increase medical school seats for students of African descent. This changes yearly and should be clearly available on their websites. If not, call the admissions department directly at the school you are applying to and ask.

Students with Disabilities

Some schools have started to catch up with the times and give students with disabilities the chance to apply in a separate stream to medical school. This means your application may not be compared to the thousands of applications in a computer system that spits out a rank and decides if you get an interview based on your grades. This usually means someone actually sits down and reviews your application in more detail. You will need to provide them with official documentation of your disability. I only found a few schools that have this separate stream for those with disabilities. Most schools don't differentiate which is disappointing as it is much harder for a student with a disability to perform on the same playing field as those without disabilities. Again contact the medical schools directly if there is nothing on their website about these special considerations.

Mature students

Should I apply? Heck Yes! Students in their 50's go to medical school.

You have to decide how many working years you have left for the 4 years you're going to spend in medical school. There is the 4 years of medical school and 2 years of residency if you want to do family medicine. If you were 40 when you got in you would be done at 46 to be come a family doctor. You must take into account your family situation. However, if you want it bad enough and you believe you can do it, go for it.

Don't let age become a barrier or worse yet another excuse for you not to reach for your dreams. You can pay your debt off pretty quickly when you're done residency. A family doctor can make between $150,000 to $650,000 if they are working 5 days a week.

I've always been a believer in accomplishing your goals no matter what your age. Don't let this be a hurdle. You only have one life. If you want something, go out and get it.

Chapter 18 - Medical school You did it!

So you're in - now what?

Celebrate! Go party, hug your family, hug yourself, go on that trip you always wanted to! Get those few things you always wanted. You have accomplished something amazing. If you don't celebrate now, you're brain and body will never work as hard next time because it won't believe your lies. If you said when I get into MD school I'm going to go to Italy, go to Italy! Please celebrate - you deserve it. Please don't prepare for medical school and study anatomy or something ridiculous. If you were registered in a research project - say I'm really sorry - but I need to back out. I need a break. Some of you will be - angry at the thought of this, but this is up to you.

You're not going to get many breaks from now on, so trust me, cherish everyone you get and enjoy it. Don't fill it with things you don't need to do. Just like all the crap people told you about getting into medical school, it's 95% gossiping. When you get your acceptance letter, do nothing, just relax, read those books you always wanted to read, travel, go to the gym, play sports, draw, write a song, do something you WANT to do!

Don't buy any text books before you get in or in the first month, UNLESS they are REQUIRED. I'm not sure if many medical schools require text books anymore. Ours didn't have a single required textbook throughout the four years. Fifteen percent of you are going to listen, the rest are going to buy the books because they make you feel better, they are going to sit on your shelf and then you're going to give them away when you go to residency because now they are a burden and out of date. I did this and so did the majority of my classmates.

If you need to buy books, buy used books from residents selling them, or fourth year medical students dumping or leaving them at your student lounge before they travel away for their residency programs. You don't need to buy any books except the ones I recommend later in this chapter. Feel free to test my theory, not with 1st or 2nd year MD students but with 4th year students and residents that are at the tail end of their training. They will give you honest advice with some perspective.

Be open minded - medical school may not be what you expected

Medical school is not everything you expect. Nothing in life ever is. It will not teach you everything about everything, and please don't go into medical school or even apply to medical school if you think it will. Medical school is there to teach you how to learn medicine and become a proficient medical doctor. It teaches you how to gather information efficiently, synthesize it, and then respond to the task at hand. This could be in a group learning environment or at the bedside in the Emergency room when you're evaluating a trauma.

Medical school has changed considerably in the past 25 years, especially the past 10 years. Since the millennium, many schools are trying to breed mature learners. Those that have less and less classroom time and more independent study time mixed in with group learning. This means a typical medical school like UBC in Vancouver that has more didactic learning and say a typical week of 20 hours of lectures, plus 9 hours of group study (PBL, CBL, PRO-COMP), 3 hours of clinical skills, and 4 hours of elective time. Thats a total of 37 hours a week on average. Dalhousie on the other coast in Halifax has 4 hours of lecture time, 8 hours of group study, 3 hours of clinical skills, and 4 hours of elective time for a total of 19 hours a week. WOW what a difference you're thinking? Now you're saying I want to go to Halifax? Maybe.. but you better be willing to pick up the slack.

These two different schools of thought are in constant battle over which one is better. LMCC examinations (your exam at the end of medical school which you write with all other Canadian Medical Students) show no statistically significant differences. Now the next couple of sentences are going to make you laugh. If you're BOOK SMART (not LIFE SMART) enough to be able to choose your school of choice then you can decide. If you're like the rest of us "normal people", then you're going go where ever you get in. In summary, if you're a driven, self motivated, mature learner - then choose a McMaster or Dalhousie medical school. If you're someone who likes to be spoon fed like high school and undergrad, where you have hours and hours of assignments and lectures, but that makes you feel smart and good about yourself, then go to a school like University of British Columbia. Fact is even these schools are changing. With new administrators and deans each medical school evolves and changes slightly. At the end of the day you wanted to be a doctor and getting into a Canadian medical school will make you an excellent doctor.

Books to buy

<u>Toronto Notes.</u> This is a comprehensive guide to almost all specialties. I used it from 1st year onwards.

<u>The Edmonton Manual.</u> An OSCE study guide. Don't really need this until 2nd year of medical school, but it is very helpful with giving you an approach to specific concerns. This book is organized by specialty and then topics within that specialty. For example you could have an OSCE station on Pelvic Bleeding which would be under the section "Obstetrics and Gynecology". In one page this manual will walk you through the relevant questions to ask on history and physical. It will include red flag symptoms, investigations, and blood work. It was my "go to" book for studying for the OSCE at the end of medical school.

<u>The Essentials of Clinical Examination Handbook</u>. This is another Toronto based book. It is one of the most comprehensive books I have seen. I would not buy the Bates - physical exam. You can't carry it around, and this book is very detailed and some great pearls. Everyone I suggested the book to used it and loved it.

Yup that's it, the rest of the information you are going to find online first, then your library if you need the books. So here is a list of online resources.

Youtube

I used Youtube and still do to learn and explain topics to patients. It sometimes take a few extra minutes to find exactly what you're looking for, but so does going to get your textbook and searching the index, then finding you what you need, and finally falling asleep because its so boring and dry. That was also time consuming... That's why videos are great because you can choose what format you like better. When you're studying for an exam and getting tired, videos have a way of keeping your attention. They have text, audio, and video, stimulating different parts of your brain. This helps keep you awake and engaged. That's why TV can keep you awake so late even when you don't love what you're watching or your exhausted.

Other Online Options

Khan Academy - great medicine videos, and now they have an entire series for the MCAT which is supported by the AAMC who created and distribute the MCAT exam.

Medical channels - subscribe to a bunch of medical channels that you like. I'd list them here but there are too many. Some have annoying voices and jokes, others are too dry. You have to find what works for you.

Dr. Najeeb Lectures - Caveat this guy has a heavy Indian accent, lectures are long and drawn out - but dammit you will understand topics. It is cheap and he covers almost every major disease that medical students need to know. He takes every topic from the basics to the bedside. It is awesome. I should credit Dr. Najeeb for some of my degree, but putting him in this book is credit enough. Trust me this is a great resource - you just need to put him on in the morning, lunch breaks, at night and you are going to kill it. Some people tried to keep this resource a secret during medical school because it was so good, but you know how I feel about secrets. I'm all about crushing secrets and giving you everything you need to know so that all you need to do is work hard.

FTP lectures - Another great resource. Videos on all the major topics on your LMCC or USMLE. The physician does an excellent job explaining topics in a simple manner. He uses the whiteboard to help with topics. You can youtube some of his videos to get an idea of how he teaches.

Chapter 19 - Residency

There are many residency programs to choose from. My favourite still is Family Medicine. It is the shortest program with the most flexibility. It is very rare to hear of a family doctor looking for work. However, if you are an orthopaedic surgeon who just graduated in 2014, you would most likely be out of a job and making no money. Many specialties are like this today as they are training the same number of residents but there are fewer jobs as the baby boomer physicians have not retired yet. The waitlists are huge, but the governments don't want to hire more doctors as that means they need to pay them more.

Family medicine also has a variety of options. One can do an additional year of emergency medicine, where you can obtain the skills to work as an ER doctor. Other "Plus 1" years include: sports medicine, anesthesia, palliative care, dermatology, research, women health, obstetrics, and more are being developed.

The flexibility of family medicine is special. A family doctor trained in Calgary can finish residency and travel to Nova Scotia, Rural Ontario, or Vancouver, and set up a clinic and start working. There are also plenty of family doctors offices looking for doctors to join their practise. Family doctors can set up their own schedules. Some work mornings and weekends so they can see their children on weeknights and their partner takes over on weekends. Others work 2 days a week. The options are limitless.

If you want to learn more about residency and specialities I suggest you get into medical school first. Do you're first years of medical school and then start to decide what you want to do. Don't think about residency yet if you aren't even in medical school.

Chapter 20 - VACATION! Summers & time between medical school and residency

I'm a believer in self care. That means doing the things you love throughout medical school and residency. "But I don't have time, and you told me to give it your all". Yes, but you can find 3-5 hours a week (at least) to focus on your hobbies, playing the guitar, going to the gym, cooking healthy meals, joining an ultimate frisbee intramural league, etc.

I recommend that all medical students take their summers (if they are in a 4 year Medical school program, sorry to you 3 year programmers - you don't have a choice) and enjoy them. That means doing things you love. Maybe you didn't get a chance to go to Italy, or travel to Thailand, perhaps you wanted to sail off the pacific coast. Whatever it is, use this time in the summers to have fun, relax your mind, and rejuvenate. You only have the summer of first and second year to enjoy (approximately 2.5 months each). In third year most schools go full time for 12-13 months taking you directly into fourth year.

At the end of fourth year you will write your MCCQE1 and then graduate from medical school. You will then have 6 weeks until July 1st to enjoy your time before you become a resident. This time is again to relax, travel, do whatever you like - just don't do academics. Please. You're body and brain need a break and a well deserved one after all that you have asked of your mind to do over the past 8 to 10 years of undergraduate degrees and medical school.

Here is a list of things my friends and I did in medical school during our time off.

- Travel
- Ski trips/ Bike Trips
- Write a book
- Paint
- Play music
- Journal
- Volunteer
- Read
- Dance
- Play sports
- Get married
- Visit family and loved ones

Chapter 21 You're done!

Now this is my favourite chapter. For many of you're reading it as a "pre-med" student. I'd love for you to circle this chapter and re-read it when you complete medical school. I want you to look back at all you have done and be proud of your accomplishments. I know I am proud of you.

Through you reading this book I know that you were challenged and had many times where you agreed and disagreed with me. That's what I wanted. I wanted to get you angry, excited, emotional, and focused. I know you picked this book up one day when you wanted to get help achieving your dream. When you wanted to reach for something and needed some guidance. I hope this book helped you see that anything is possible.

I spent a lot of this book talking about motivation and providing you with messages like "go for your dreams", "believe in yourself", "never give up", and "sharpen your axe". The purpose for all that is to show you how much confidence you have deep inside you that is unawakened. It's like a beautiful sunny day sitting inside you waiting for you to just open those curtains and shine bright. You are that amazing and I have faith that you will one day see it, if you have not already done so. The rest of this book was full of details to help you on your way.

I want you to know that I have faith in you, I have always had faith in you, even though I don't know you. How can I say such a thing? Because we are more similar than you think.

I can't wait to hear your dreams and accomplishments. I promise I'll email you back or maybe even call you if you get into medical school. I'll be as happy as you and I'm thankful and honoured that you let me join you on your journey.

Congratulations my friend, you've embarked on a journey that will help you, your parents, your kids, your patients, and the communities you will work in.

From my heart to yours,

GO FOR YOUR DREAMS, THEY ARE WAITING FOR YOU.

DR. NORRY KALER MD

49262399R00089

6Made in the USA
Charleston, SC
22 November 2015